T0388608

Dialogic Collaborative Action Research in Science Education

This engaging and practical book offers science teacher educators and K-12 science teachers alike the tools to engage in a dialogic mode of collaborative action research (D-CAR), a collaborative mode of action research focused on teachers' experiences with students, reflection upon these experiences, and peer learning.

Renowned science educator Allan Feldman and co-authors from across numerous settings in K-12 science education present the theory, methodology, case studies, and practical advice to support the use of D-CAR as a means to enhance teachers' normal practice and address the problems, dilemmas, and dissonances that science teachers must negotiate as they work to meet the needs of an increasingly diverse student population and engage with complex science teaching challenges that disproportionately affect marginalized students.

The book will be of use to science teacher educators, pre-service and in-service science teachers, professional development specialists, or any science educator invested in developing creative, reflective, and thoughtful teachers.

Allan Feldman is Emeritus Professor of Science Education in the College of Education at the University of South Florida, USA.

Jawaher Alsultan is Assistant Professor of Curriculum and Instruction; Science Education in the College of Education at Imam Abdulrahman Bin Faisal University in Dammam, Saudi Arabia.

Katie Laux is Assistant Professor of Education at Upper Iowa University, USA.

Molly Nation is Associate Professor of Environmental Education in the Department of Ecology and Environmental Studies at Florida Gulf Coast University, USA.

Teaching and Learning in Science Series
Judith S. Lederman and Reneé Schwartz, Series Editors

Representations of Nature of Science in School Science Textbooks
A Global Perspective
Edited by Christine V. McDonald, Fouad Abd-El-Khalick

Teaching Biology in Schools
Global Research, Issues, and Trends
Edited by Kostas Kampourakis, Michael Reiss

Theory and Methods for Sociocultural Research in Science and Engineering Education
Edited by Gregory J. Kelly and Judith Green

Supporting Self-Directed Learning in Science and Technology
Beyond the School Years
Edited by Léonie Rennie, Susan M. Stocklmayer, and John K. Gilbert

Sensemaking in Elementary Science
Supporting Teacher Learning
Edited by Elizabeth A. Davis, Carla Zembal-Saul and Sylvie M. Kademian

Discourse Strategies for Science Teaching and Learning
Research and Practice
Kok-Sing Tang

Handbook of Research on Science Education
Volume III
Edited by Norman G. Lederman, Dana L. Zeidler, and Judith S. Lederman

Dialogic Collaborative Action Research in Science Education
Collaborative Conversations for Improving Science Teaching and Learning
Allan Feldman, Jawaher Alsultan, Katie Laux, and Molly Nation

For more information about this series, please visit: https://www.routledge.com/Teaching-and-Learning-in-Science-Series/book-series/LEATLSS

Dialogic Collaborative Action Research in Science Education
Collaborative Conversations for Improving Science Teaching and Learning

Allan Feldman, Jawaher Alsultan, Katie Laux, and Molly Nation

Routledge
Taylor & Francis Group

NEW YORK AND LONDON

Designed cover image: © Getty Images

First published 2024
by Routledge
605 Third Avenue, New York, NY 10158

and by Routledge
4 Park Square, Milton Park, Abingdon, Oxon OX14 4RN

Routledge is an imprint of the Taylor & Francis Group, an informa business

© 2024 Allan Feldman, Jawaher Alsultan, Katie Laux, and Molly Nation

ISBN: 978-1-032-30896-8 (hbk)
ISBN: 978-1-032-30895-1 (pbk)
ISBN: 978-1-003-30717-4 (ebk)

DOI: 10.4324/9781003307174

Typeset in Galliard
by Taylor & Francis Books

Contents

List of illustrations   viii

1 Introduction to the Book   1

   Introducing Ourselves 1
   Our Approach to Action Research 4
   D-CAR and Wicked Problems 6
   How to Engage in D-CAR in a Nutshell 6
   Overview of the Book 8
   Summary 8
   References 9

2 The Principles of Action Research   11

   Introduction 11
   History of Action Research 11
   What is Action Research? 12
   Characteristics of Action Research 13
   Action Research and Constructivism 16
   Action Research in Science Education 18
   Summary 24
   References 24

3 Introduction to Dialogic Collaborative Action Research
  (D-CAR)   31

   Introduction 31
   Collaboration 31
   Collaborative Action Research 33
   The Nature of Dialogue 35
   Dialogic Collaborative Action Research (D-CAR) 36

Summary 39
Note 39
References 39

4 Wicked Problems in Science Education 43

Introduction 43
Characteristics of Wicked Problems 44
Wicked Problems in Science Education 47
Summary 51
Note 51
References 51

5 How to Implement D-CAR 55

Introduction 55
Starting a D-CAR Group 55
Being Collaborative 56
Methods for Creating Dialogic Conversations 57
Including Students/Student Voice in Research 73
Facilitators and Critical Friends 75
Summary 78
Notes 78
References 79

6 Engaging in Conventional Action Research 83

Introduction 83
Finding a Starting Point for Research 83
Developing a Research Question 84
Types of Data 85
Ladder of Inference 86
Data 87
Developing a Data Collection Plan 93
Collecting Data – Informed Consent 94
Analyzing Data 95
Summary 103
References 103

7 Barriers to Implementing Action Research 105

Introduction 105
Deprofessionalization of Teaching 105

Constraints on Science Teachers' Time 108
Difficulties in Changing One's Practice 109
What About Professional Development (PD) Programs? 110
Summary 112
References 112

8   Extending the Conversation – Making D-CAR Public   114

Introduction 114
Importance of Sharing Conversations and Knowledge 114
Sharing for Professional, Personal, and Political Purposes of Action
  Research 115
Sharing to Contribute to Knowledge Democracy 118
Methods of Sharing 120
Summary 125
Note 125
References 125

9   Cases of D-CAR   129

Introduction 129
Action Research to Address Non-Wicked Problems in Science
  Education 129
Action Research to Address Wicked Problems in Science
  Education 132
Summary 141
Note 141
References 142

10 Afterword   144

Index   146

Illustrations

Figures

2.1 The action research cycle. 15
5.1 Structure of the Physics Teachers Action Research Group (PTARG). 57
5.2 The Dialogos Method of having conversations. 60
5.3 An example of a lesson study process. 62
5.4 Example of the use of a fishbone diagram. 69
5.5 An example of a student's science teaching autobiography. 70
5.6 A second example of a student's science teaching autobiography. 71
5.7 Hierarchy of student participation developed by Katie. 74
6.1 The ladder of inference. 86
6.2 An example of how to represent student data graphically using a scatterplot. 98
6.3 An example of how to represent student data graphically using a column chart. 98
6.4. An example of how to represent average data graphically. 99

Table

6.1 Pre- and posttest student test scores. 96

1 Introduction to the Book

Introducing Ourselves

As we write this book, we wonder who you are, the person who has picked it up and begun to read it. We're hoping you are a practicing science teacher who wants to improve your practice and the educational situation within which it is immersed. You might be someone involved in informal science education and you work at a zoo, museum, aquarium, nature center, or with groups like the Boy Scouts, Girl Scouts, Boy and Girls Clubs, or any other ways people are engaged in learning science outside of formal schooling. It's also possible you are a science teacher educator, someone whose practice is to help prepare new science teachers or to guide experienced teachers as they seek to improve their practice, or to study the ways in which science teachers learn to teach. We believe no matter who you are in relation to science education, you will find this book to be both useful and enlightening.

While we would need a crystal ball to know who you are, we can help you get to know us by providing some background about how we are involved in science teacher action research, and how that came about. To make this more personable, we will tell our stories in the first person. We'll start with Allan, who has had the longest experience with action research.

Allan's Association with Action Research

My explicit connection to action research began in 1989 when I stopped being a science teacher after 17 years and began full-time study for my doctorate. I was privileged to be able to do my doctoral work with some of the leading scholars in teacher education, including my advisor, Mike Atkin. I don't remember when we first began to talk about action research, but I believe during my first semester I did a literature review of action research as an independent study with Mike. As I was reading about what it was, I began to realize that I was somewhat of an action researcher when I was a science teacher. I tried out new teaching ideas, I thought deeply about them, I shared them with my colleagues at conferences of the American Association of Physics Teachers (AAPT), and even published some of my ideas in *The Physics Teacher*

DOI: 10.4324/9781003307174-1

(Feldman, 1981a, 1984, 1991), and in a small journal published by the school where I taught (Feldman, 1981b, 1985, 1988). What I didn't do is to engage in the process we refer to in this book as conventional action research. I didn't identify a research question, collect data, analyze data, or use that analysis to inform my practice.

As a doctoral student in science teacher education, I also read the literature on teachers and teacher education. My biggest surprise was that I didn't see myself or my teaching colleagues in that literature. The primary research paradigm at that time looked at the effects of teaching practices and rarely included any information about the teachers themselves. When the teachers were described, they were not the reflective, engaged, professionals who I worked with in public and private schools. I began to realize that action research would be a way to engage with science teachers and decided for my dissertation to convene a group of physics teachers who would engage in action research, and to study how they learned from each other and how that affected their practice (Feldman, 1996). It was as a result of this study I began to explore the use of dialogue in action research. In later chapters of this book we return to the story of the Physics Teachers Action Research Group (PTARG), which is what the group called itself.

I was also lucky in my doctoral studies that my advisor was in close contact with a group of researchers in the UK who were instrumental in the resurgence of action research both in the UK and in Europe (Feldman, 2017). Among them was Peter Posch, who was on sabbatical at my university and was writing the first English edition of Teachers Investigate Their Work (Altrichter et al., 1993) while I was studying what was happening with PTARG. Since then I have taught classes on doing action research, facilitated groups of science teachers as they engaged in action research, and did action research on my own practice as a science teacher educator and facilitator of action research. I've also had the opportunity to work with doctoral students who had an interest in action research. My co-authors of this book all did their doctoral work under my supervision. We will hear from them next.

Jawaher's Connection with Action Research

My connection with action research started after finishing my bachelor's degree, where I worked as a physics teacher at a private school in Saudi Arabia. While there, other science teachers and I met weekly with the science department supervisor to discuss our struggles and success, provide each other with advice, and share materials. These meetings opened our horizons to how we can enhance students' desire and passion for the science field. Together we learned fundamental strategies of teaching and learning through attending workshops, observing each other's classrooms, and designing after-school activities. Through the years I worked in public and private schools, where I continued creating communities of science teachers and maintaining my connection with previous ones. Back then, I did not know the appropriate terminology for these meetings. The first time I was introduced to action research terminology was during the first year of my doctorate program. I had the privilege to work with Allan on several research projects that focused on science teachers conducting action research. For example, we worked with ten high school science teachers to support them in finding ways to engage their students online in inquiry, discussion, and argumentation at the beginning of the COVID-19 pandemic.

Another example is when we engaged middle school math and science teachers in action research to develop methods and materials to deliver high-quality, reform-based instruction through online platforms. The purpose was to increase students' knowledge of public health issues and their ability to serve their communities as COVID-19 public health ambassadors. Similarly, in my dissertation, I recruited four high school science teachers from large school districts in the eastern region of Saudi Arabia. They participated virtually in digital game-based learning professional development (DGBL-PD), which consisted of five training sessions during the summer of 2020 and three community of practice meetings and teachers' action research presentations during the fall of 2020. We will discuss each of these projects later in the book. My work with Allan was somewhat different from what I read in the action research literature as it was focused on the enhancement of the teachers' daily practice rather than teachers' implementation of social science research.

After earning my doctorate, I continued my connection with action research by facilitating several communities of practice for in-service science teachers as well as being a member of The Professional Fellowship in University Teaching and Learning program team at Imam Abdulrahman Bin Faisal University, which is an academic-year professional development (PD) program intended to advance teaching and learning knowledge, skills, and practice for university educators, leading to the recognition of outstanding teaching and learning practices in Saudi higher education. One essential step of this program is for faculty members to conduct and present their action research that focuses on solving dilemmas encountered in teaching and learning practices.

Katie's Involvement in Action Research

After four years of teaching middle school science, I left public education to focus on my doctoral studies. I first learned about action research after taking a course with Allan. He eventually became my advisor as well. When I was first learning about action research, I did not understand why there was not more of a focus on this in the K-12 setting as it seemed like it would have great benefits for both teachers and students. At the same time, I also became interested in student voice. This led to my dissertation, which focused on me working with high school science teachers as they engaged in action research with the goal of promoting student voice in their classrooms.

As a graduate student, I worked on projects that included action research in the design. For example, along with Allan and Molly, I engaged in dialogic collaborative action research (D-CAR) with marine science teachers as they attempted to include more inquiry, discussion, and argumentation into their classes. After graduation, I worked as a science administrator at Hillsborough County Public Schools in Florida, and facilitated action research groups with science and math teachers as they attempted to improve their practice through discussions of equity and inclusion of students in science, technology, engineering, and mathematics (STEM).

In my current role as an assistant professor of education at Upper Iowa University, I use action research principles with my classes. I teach them activities such as analytic discourse (see Chapter 5) that they can use with other teachers in their professional learning communities (PLCs). I am currently beginning an action research project where I will reflect on how I encourage student voice in my classes and how this benefits my students.

Molly's Relationship with Action Research

I am currently an associate professor of environmental education in The Water School at Florida Gulf Coast University. Before getting my doctorate in science education, I was a middle and high school science teacher. I now use that experience to engage K-12 educators in environmentally focused curriculum. I have focused my scholarly efforts to promote climate change education in my teaching and with professional development (PD) of K-12 educators. Through collaborative action research and creating communities of practice, I align education and research to promote the practice of teaching and learning science. Controversy and public debates surrounding issues such as climate change have led to mistrust around science and science education. This was a big part of my dissertation, and I have written about it in the journal *Science & Education* (Nation & Feldman, 2022). Through my dissertation work (Nation, 2017), I found teachers wanted to engage their students in discussions and argumentation when teaching global climate change (GCC), but were reluctant to because they were concerned about curricular time constraints, were reluctant to give up control of the classroom, and were unsure how to do it properly. Engaging in D-CAR in a friendly, supportive environment helped the participants to assuage their concerns and learn how to engage their students in discussion and argumentation. The PD designed as a result of these findings was focused on incorporating inquiry, discussion, and argumentation into the marine science classroom as part of the existing curriculum.

Our Approach to Action Research

You may already be familiar with the idea of action research. To us, its purpose is to investigate your own practice and practice situation in order to improve either or both, and to produce new understandings that can be shared with other science teachers. In most books or articles about action research it is described in a way that is similar to academic research in the social sciences. It begins with the identification of some type of problem the science teacher would want to address or solve; the collection of preliminary data that can be used to develop an action plan; the implementation of that plan along with the collection of data about its effects; and analysis of the data, which then leads to modifications in the action plan and so on. We refer to this model of action research as *conventional action research* (see Chapter 6 for information about how to do conventional action research). We call it conventional for two reasons. First, conventional is usually taken to mean traditional, usual, standard, or normal. Conventional action research is simply our way of stating the usual way that action research is depicted and presented to practitioners. Conventional can also mean "relating to convention or general agreement; established by social convention; having its origin or sanction merely in an artificial convention of any kind; arbitrarily or artificially determined" (Oxford English Dictionary, 2022). This is our second reason for using the adjective "conventional" – the reason that action research is formulated in this way is because it has been agreed upon, either explicitly or implicitly, to consist of doing these steps.

Conventional can also mean conformist, predictable, or unadventurous. Our approach to action research is non-traditional, adventurous, non-conformist, and possibly unpredictable. We call it *dialogic collaborative action research*, or D-CAR. Rather than focusing on a particular way to do research, as does conventional action research, we focus on what can happen when a group of science teachers get together to talk with one another about their teaching and educational situations and how to make changes and improve them. D-CAR draws on the power of conversation as research (Feldman, 1999) and the power of the crowd (Landemore, 2012) to share and construct knowledge. In addition, it is better than conventional action research at meeting the immediate needs of teachers and the rhythm of teaching.

D-CAR does the above by building on the long tradition of the accumulation and construction of knowledge by craftspeople. For thousands of years, knowledge of how rather than knowledge of what or why was accumulated by artisans who engaged in practices such as metallurgy, architecture, cooking, engineering, and medicine. Often the knowledge generated by trying things out was shared within workshops and guilds, but also shared among practitioners, which led to the knowledge of how to, for example, cast a metal lizard or set a broken bone (Grafton, 2022), being distributed and improved upon by other practitioners. The same has been true for science teachers. Knowledge of teaching science has been developed by individual teachers. Often that knowledge has stayed with the science teacher. Sometimes it is shared with other teachers in the school, with a student teacher, or more rarely in workshops, presentations, or publications. Therefore, among science teachers most of the knowledge of how to teach science remains with individual teachers or is shared locally. D-CAR encourages the sharing within a group, which leads to the trying out of this knowledge by other teachers, and the construction of new knowledge by the group. It also encourages the sharing of the knowledge beyond the group, because as Lawrence Stenhouse (1981) argued, for an activity to be defined as research, its results must be made public.

D-CAR and Wicked Problems

Before we give an overview of how to engage in D-CAR, we want to make clear that we believe this process can assist science teachers to go beyond the technical problems of teaching to help to alleviate or mitigate the "wicked problems" of education (more information about wicked problems can be found in Chapter 4). Wicked problems are ones that are too complicated to define or describe explicitly, and do not have straightforward or clear-cut solutions (Rittel & Webber, 1973). Wicked problems permeate all aspects of science teachers' practice. For example, issues of class, race, ethnicity, gender, and socio-economic status affect our schools, individual students, and their communities. These issues are tied together tightly and loosely, and affect how we teach and how students learn. Clearly no one science teacher can solve wicked problems like these. But when working together in groups, they can help alleviate or mitigate them locally.

The role of science teachers in helping to alleviate wicked educational problems begins with their classroom practice, shared and critiqued with other teachers, and made public. This happens in D-CAR when it is employed by science teachers to construct and share knowledge about how to teach, and is then shared more broadly through workshops, presentations, blogs, websites, articles, and even books. But as Smith (2022) noted, for other science teachers to be successful in implementing this new and shared knowledge requires time and practice doing so in their own classrooms. This is how we see the role of D-CAR in helping to alleviate educational wicked problems.

How to Engage in D-CAR in a Nutshell

In Chapters 5–8 we go into details about establishing a D-CAR group, how to engage in conversations as research, ways to address possible barriers, and making your research public. In this section of this introductory chapter we provide a brief overview of the D-CAR process.

Establishing a D-CAR Group

An important early step in the D-CAR process is to find a number of like-minded science teachers to form a collaborative group. You can do this either before or after you identify an issue, problem, dilemma, or dissonance in your practice that you want to address. If you start with the issue then you would need to find other science teachers who share that concern. Or you could begin by convening a group of teachers who have as their goal to improve their science teaching. The teachers may be from within one school, or from multiple schools. We've found that a good way to recruit teachers is to make presentations at workshops or local conferences. Personal connections are particularly effective – you invite teachers you know and they invite ones they know. In the past D-CAR groups have met face-to-face. This can still be an option, but as video conferencing technology has improved, we've seen that virtual meetings can be very effective. For D-CAR groups that go beyond one school, virtual meetings eliminate travel time, and can better fit into teachers' busy schedules.

Conversations as Research

The power of D-CAR is in the use of conversations as a research method. Allan first saw this when working with the physics teachers in PTARG, and then explored it in his teaching of action research (Feldman, 1998). We go into how and why conversations can be a research methodology in Chapter 3 and provide many ways to engage in conversations in Chapter 5. When you engage in conversation as a research methodology, you need to provide a structure that transforms it from chit-chat or "shooting the breeze." This can be done with an agenda for the meeting the group agrees on; having a mechanism for keeping track of what was said, shared, and decided upon; and a set of norms to guide how the group functions.

Making Research Public

As we noted above, making your research public is a fundamental aspect of D-CAR (see Chapter 8). This happens at several levels. First, because you are not going alone with this, your research group itself serves as the first level at which you are sharing your work. You can do this by sharing short stories or anecdotes about your teaching that illuminates your concerns or provide details about ideas that you've tried out to improve your teaching or educational situation. In doing so, the other members of your group provide constructive critique, learn about what you're doing, and gain ideas about what they can do to improve their practice or educational situations. The other levels are distinguished by the audience and the formality of how you report what you've learned. In the US, secondary science teachers are usually part of a science department. If this is the case for you, then you can report what you've learned to the rest of your department, either in a formal or informal presentation. Most school districts in the US have opportunities for teachers to present or run workshops. In many areas there are local or regional science teacher associations that are prime venues to share your work. It's also possible for you and your group to present at national conferences. Finally, you can share your work via the Internet or print science teacher journals.

The Possibility of Conventional Action Research

As you'll see as you read this book, we believe that D-CAR can serve the needs of science teachers to work together to improve their practice and educational situations, and generate new knowledge and understanding about the teaching and learning of science. However, you may find the desire or need to use the methods of conventional action research. One reason may be that you want to dig deeper into the issues and feel that gathering certain data will give you a better sense of what's happening in your classroom, school, or community. Another reason, which we discuss in Chapter 8, is that among many policy makers and administrators, teachers' knowledge does not have the same legitimacy as knowledge produced by university researchers. Engaging in conventional action research could convince them otherwise.

Overview of the Book

In this book, we move the thinking of action research beyond the conventional by shifting from the use of social sciences' demanding methods to highlighting the importance of dialogue among science teachers seeking to improve science teaching and learning. We now provide an overview of what you will find in the rest of this book.

The primary goal of Chapter 2 is to provide readers with foundational knowledge about action research and an overview of the different ways it has been conceptualized and implemented in science education. Chapter 3 presents our view of action research, D-CAR. D-CAR relies on the power of structured conversations among small groups of science teachers to go beyond the solving of day-to-day technical problems engaging with complex and unclear issues in teaching science, including wicked problems. Chapter 4 further explores how D-CAR can help you to alleviate or mitigate the wicked problems in science education you face in your educational situations.

Chapter 5 gives guidance about how to develop a D-CAR group, and how the group can initiate and sustain dialogue among its members. The purpose of Chapter 6 is to provide information and methods for when science teachers want to or are required to gather and analyze data by engaging in conventional action research. Conventional action research requires significant time commitments from science teachers as well as learning the methods of the social sciences; therefore, in this chapter, we describe the process in detail step by step.

In Chapter 7, we address some of the obstacles to integrating conventional action research including deprofessionalization of teaching, the difficulty in changing practice, and time constraints; and how we can mitigate them using D-CAR. In Chapter 8 we explore how you can make your knowledge public. Chapter 9 provides examples of science teacher action research that used conversations and dialogues as a primary research method.

Summary

Our purposes in this chapter were to introduce readers to us, the authors of this book, and to what makes our approach to action research, D-CAR, different from other more conventional forms. We began with our stories and how we were introduced to action research and made use of it in our practice as well as with practicing science teachers. As we're sure you've seen, our stories are not much different from those of other science educators. We also sought to begin to familiarize readers with the advantages of using the D-CAR approach, especially for helping to mitigate the wicked problems faced by science teachers. Finally, we provided readers with the nutshell version of D-CAR to serve as an advance organizer (Ausubel et al., 1978) so that the ideas we present later in the book have a cognitive framework to hang on. We believe it is also important for readers to know some of the history of action research in science education. Therefore, we turn to that in the next chapter.

References

Altrichter, H., Posch, P., & Somekh, B. (1993). *Teachers investigate their work: An introduction to the methods of action research.* New York and Abingdon, UK: Routledge.

Ausubel, D. P., Hanesian, H., Novak, J. D., & Hanesian, H. (1978). *Educational psychology: A cognitive view* (2nd edition). New York: Holt, Rinehart and Winston.

Feldman, A. (1981a). A model of the Savery steam engine. *The Physics Teacher*, 19(6), 414–415. doi:10.1119/1.2340832.

Feldman, A. (1981b). The need for science education. *Studies in Education*, 42, 3–9.

Feldman, A. (1984). Using space shuttle launch data in the physics classroom. *The Physics Teacher*, 22(1), 30–31. doi:10.1119/1.2341447.

Feldman, A. (1985). Teaching in science classes about nuclear weapons and war. *Studies in Education*, 50, 32–37.

Feldman, A. (1988). Contemporary physics: A new physics program at GFS. *Studies in Education*, 54, 16–20.

Feldman, A. (1991). The speed of light in different media. *The Physics Teacher*, 29(2), 112–112. doi:10.1119/1.2343234.

Feldman, A. (1996). Enhancing the practice of physics teachers: Mechanisms for the generation and sharing of knowledge and understanding in collaborative action research. *Journal of Research in Science Teaching*, 33(5), 513–540. doi:10.1002/(SICI)1098-2736(199605)33:5<513:AID-TEA4>3.0.CO;2-U.

Feldman, A. (1998). Implementing and assessing the power of conversation in the teaching of action research. *Teacher Education Quarterly*, 25(2), 27–42.

Feldman, A. (1999). The role of conversation in collaborative action research. *Educational Action Research*, 7(1), 125–144.

Feldman, A. (2017). An emergent history of educational action research in the English-speaking world. In L. L. Rowell, C. D. Bruce, J. M. Shosh, & M. M. Riel (eds.), *The Palgrave international handbook of action research* (pp. 125–145). New York: Springer.

Grafton, A. (2022). How to cast a metal lizard. *New York Review of Books*, 69(14), 41–43.

Landemore, H. (2012). Collective wisdom: Old and new. In H. Landemore & J. Elster (eds.), *Collective wisdom: Principles and mechanisms* (pp. 1–20). Cambridge: Cambridge University Press. doi:10.1017/CBO9780511846427.001.

Nation, M. T. (2017). *How teachers' beliefs about climate change influence their instruction, student understanding, and willingness to take action*. Dissertation, University of South Florida, Tampa, FL. https://search.proquest.com/docview/1949401046?accountid=14745.

Nation, M. T., & Feldman, A. (2022). Climate change and political controversy in the science classroom. *Science & Education*, 31(6), 1567–1583. doi:10.1007/s11191-022-00330-6.

Oxford English Dictionary (2022). "conventional, adj. 3". Oxford University Press. Retrieved from https://www.oed.com/view/Entry/40715?redirectedFrom=conventional#eid.

Rittel, H. W. J., & Webber, M. M. (1973). Dilemmas in a general theory of planning. *Policy Sciences*, 4(2), 155–169. doi:10.1007/BF01405730.

Smith, P. H. (2022). *From lived experience to the written word: Reconstructing practical knowledge in the early modern world*. Chicago, IL: University of Chicago Press.

Stenhouse, L. (1981). What counts as research? *British Journal of Educational Studies*, 29(2), 103–114.

2 The Principles of Action Research

Introduction

Our intent in this chapter is to provide readers with an overview of the history and nature of action research. This has become more and more difficult to do as the notion of what action research is has expanded over the years, and because the number of publications about it has exploded since Allan first began to work in the field in the late 1980s. At that time an ERIC search of the term would have found hundreds of publications. The same search today results in over 12,000! A Google Scholar search found over 1.5 million hits! Clearly, we cannot include everything about action research in this chapter. Rather, we look at the field from our perspective, with a focus on action research in science education.

History of Action Research

There are a number of publications that have traced the history of action research (e.g., Feldman, 2017; Foshay, 1994; Hendricks, 2019; McTaggart, 1991). Recently, Allan published a chapter about the history of action research in the English speaking world, which appeared in *The Palgrave International Handbook of Action Research* (Feldman, 2017). As with most others, he began the history with Kurt Lewin, who first published the term "action research" in his article "Action Research and Minority Problems" (1946). To Lewin, action research was "comparative research on the conditions and effects of various forms of social action, and research leading to social action" (Lewin, 1946, p. 35). He discussed action research as a form of experimental inquiry to solve social problems and raise the level of independence, equality, and cooperation among minorities (Lewin, 1946). Consequently, his vision of action research began with taking actions, collecting data related to those actions, and ended with evaluating the action (Noffke, 1990).

Even though Lewin developed the idea of action research, it did not spring forth from a vacuum but rather drew upon the work of others. For example, in the 1920s Burdette Buckingham wrote a book titled *Research for Teachers* (Buckingham, 1926). It focused on teachers conducting case studies to make

DOI: 10.4324/9781003307174-2

public, gain knowledge, and improve the teaching profession. Similarly, John Dewey (1929) emphasized teachers' fundamental role in contributing to educational research that aims at the improvement of teaching and learning.

Although Buckingham and Dewey wrote about how teachers could engage in research on their practice, the use of action research by teachers was not popularized until the 1950s with the publication of *Action Research to Improve School Practices* (Corey, 1953). Stephen Corey described action research in this way:

> The type of research that is conducted in local situations and is designed to help the people working there know whether or not what they are doing is right is called 'action research.' The reason for the name is that the investigations are undertaken to determine the consequences of specific educational practices in actual schools.
>
> (Corey, 1949, p. 148)

He further outlined what he called the "minimum essentials of action research design" that required goal hypothesis, procedure description, data collection method, and result generalizations (Corey, 1949, p. 152). Corey's (1953) perspective of action research mainly focused on teachers' engagement in hypothesis formulation and testing. Thus, Corey's (1949) views of action research were more technical and problem-solving in comparison with Lewin's, who put more emphasis on social justice. This movement made by Corey and others to make action research more "scientific" led to the decline of the implementation of action research in the US because teachers were not able to meet the standards of scientific educational research (Feldman, 2017).

Action research had a resurgence in the 1970s in the UK under the leadership of Lawrence Stenhouse (1975) who realized the new humanities curriculum would be better implemented if teachers investigated their use of it in their classrooms. After Stenhouse's death, the British action research movement continued at the University of East Anglia with projects such as the Ford Teaching Project and the Teacher–Student Interaction and Quality of Learning Project (Elliott, 1991). John Elliott, Stenhouse, and others saw action research as a way for teachers' practice to develop through investigation of their teaching and practice situations. Action research continued to spread throughout the world during the 1980s and 1990s through the Writing Projects in the US (BAWP, 1979), as a form of emancipatory research in Australia (Carr & Kemmis, 1986; Kemmis et al., 2014), and as community-based research in the Global south (Fals-Borda, 1987).

What is Action Research?

Clearly there is more to the history of action research than the brief description above. More importantly, what is action research? To Elliott, action research is "the study of a social situation with a view to improving the quality of action within it" (Elliott, 1991, p. 69). According to Bassey (1998), the primary purpose of teachers conducting action research is to understand, evaluate, and then make changes to improve educational practice. In essence, action research is a transformative process that goes beyond changing one's practice to the transformation of thoughts, actions, and behaviors (Kemmis & McTaggart, 1986), as well as the education situation in which the practice is embedded. Wilfred Carr and Stephen Kemmis (1986) situated action research within a critical theory perspective and described it as collective, collaborative inquiry done by a self-critical community of practitioners seeking to transform the educational system by researching their own practice. For this book we use the following definition of action research, which Allan developed based on the work of Elliott (1991) and Stenhouse (1975, 1981):

> Action research happens when people are involved in researching their own practice in order to improve it and to come to a better understanding of their practice situations. It is action because they act within the systems that they are trying to improve and understand. It is research because it is systematic, critical inquiry made public.
>
> (Feldman, 2007, p. 242)

Characteristics of Action Research

Although as we noted above, there are numerous ways in which action research is described and defined – see for example the chapter "Practitioner Research" by Kenneth Zeichner and Susan Noffke (2001) – most varieties of teacher action research share several characteristics. These include its purposes, it is done by practitioners, it is collaborative, it is cyclical in nature, and it should be made public.

Purposes of Action Research

In our definition above we stated that science teachers and others study their practice in order to improve it and to come to a better understanding of their practice situations. These purposes could be very specific – for example, to determine the best way to teach particular content or to implement new teaching methods, or much broader by trying to tackle one of the wicked educational problems teachers face (see Chapter 4 for more information about wicked educational problems). The purposes can also be located among three dimensions identified by Noffke (1997): the professional, personal, and/or political. Professional purposes are those that serve the profession. These include adding to the knowledge base of science teaching, the improvement of the status of teaching, and by adding to professional development (PD) efforts. Personal purposes are those in which individuals or a group of science teachers have to improve their practice or educational situations. Finally, political purposes are those that seek to change or transform the nature of teachers' work or the milieu in which children learn. Political purposes are often tied to wicked educational problems. We delve more deeply into these dimensions in Chapter 8 when we discuss the need to make action research public.

Other authors have detailed benefits of action research. For example, Valsa Koshy (2009) noted that action research is done by practitioners who are immersed in their specific context or situation. It is done continuously and modifications in both actions and methods can happen as the project progresses. As a result, "there are opportunities for theory to emerge from the research rather than always follow a previously formulated theory; the study can lead to open-ended outcomes; [and] through action research, a researcher can bring a story to life" (p. 25).

Action Research Is Done By Practitioners On and In Their Practice

As opposed to traditional forms of research, in action research the researchers are the practitioners. Thus, there is no distinction between who is a researcher and who is a practitioner. Gordon Wells (2009), reflecting on his longitudinal study in Bristol, UK, emphasized the importance of being a participant member of the classroom community to understand what happens in a particular lesson and gain the perspectives of those who are involved in it. He argued that traditional researchers inquire into others' lives as a "fly on the wall." Wells argued this method is insufficient, especially in education. Each class has its unique history, which provides a resource that participants draw on in successive lessons (Green & Dixon, 1993). Thus, it is essential to always situate action research within the real-life experiences of those who live it.

Action research rejects traditional social science research approaches in which an external researcher examines and represents what is happening in the classrooms (Wells, 2009). It is a form of research that individuals can undertake in any context, regardless of their position or status. According to Kemmis et al. (2014), the salient aspects of action research are the exceptional access practitioners have to their educational situations; how the research is conducted in the teachers' local sites; speaking the shared language of those whose action constitutes the practice being investigated; and understanding the needs of changing times and circumstances by being 'insiders'. Consequently, action research recognizes the capacity of individuals in a particular field to participate actively in all aspects of the research process to improve their practice (Feldman et al., 2018; Kemmis et al., 2014; Wells, 2009).

Action Research is Collaborative

Action research is almost always a collaborative effort among science teachers to improve their practice, build professional community, and construct knowledge in their field (Clift et al., 1990; Feldman et al., 2018; Mitchell et al., 2009). This is crucial, especially in education, because classrooms are sites of socially mediated actions, and action research leads to an in-depth understanding of self as well as the construction of new knowledge of how to negotiate these socially mediated environments. As noted by McNiff (2013), "the meaning of action research is in the way people live together" (p. 16). In action research, encounters with others are opportunities for self-learning and growth. Its quality is based on how others would benefit from their experiences and how it would improve their field.

Action Research is Cyclical

When engaging in action research we reflect, inquire, and take action (Feldman et al., 2018; Kemmis et al., 2014; McDonagh et al., 2020; McNiff, 2013; Mills, 2018). Action research is usually described as a cycle that includes planning, acting, evaluating, refining, and learning from the experience (Koshy, 2009). Because one must begin somewhere, the action research cycle usually starts with reflection by teachers on their current educational situations. However, because there needs to be something to reflect about, first teachers need to pay close attention to what they and their students do in the classroom. Elliott refers to this as reconnaissance (1991). Reflection and reconnaissance lead to the identification of problems, dilemmas, and dissonances in practice the teachers want to resolve or address. Therefore, they need to develop action plans based on those reflections and their goals. This is followed by gathering information on the impact of these actions on their practice. The teachers then reflect on this information, revise their action plans, and take new actions. This cycle is repeated until the teacher is satisfied with the results (see Figure 2.1).

For example, a science teacher might note that students encounter difficulty understanding and engaging with some science concepts or that despite all the laboratory activities done in the classroom, students do not improve their abilities to engage in scientific inquiry. After reflecting on the situation and

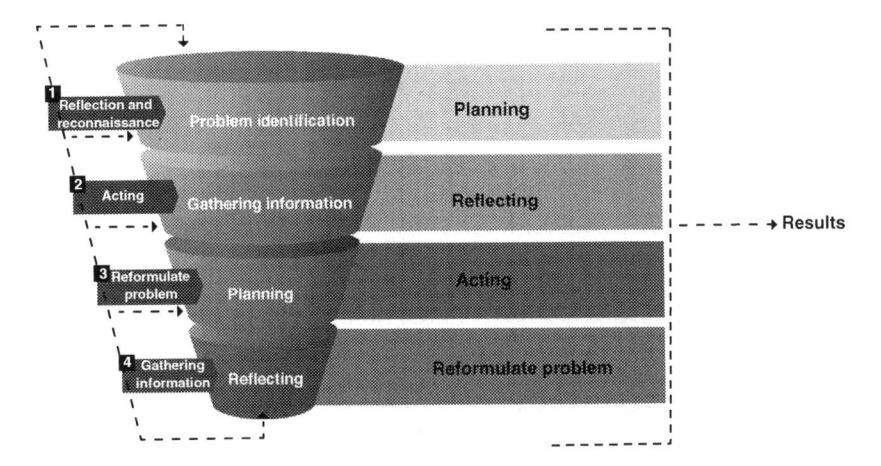

Figure 2.1 The action research cycle.

gathering some preliminary information, the science teacher action researcher would search for actions that could be taken to help resolve the issue. This search could include publications, the Internet, or asking colleagues for advice. When one considers the variety and complexity of the factors influencing what goes on in classrooms, it is not surprising that science teachers may need to implement cycles of reflection, and action, gather information about the effects of the actions, before they come to some resolution of the encountered problem. Through this process, they generate knowledge about their practice that can be shared with others and contribute to what we know about teaching and learning science

Action Researchers Make Their Research Public

Finally, as Stenhouse (1981) argued, research isn't research unless it is made public. We devote Chapter 8 to why and how the outcomes of action research should be made public. However, it is also important for the doing of action research to be open and transparent. This is because it is research in and on practice, and it is happening in the public sphere and with other teachers, administrators, students, and those stakeholders being affected by it. Therefore, it is important that action research not be a stealth activity, and all involved are informed and provide their consent if needed. In Chapter 6 we provide some information about gaining human subjects' approval from an institutional review board.

Action Research and Constructivism

Although it is possible to engage in action research without exploring the theories that underlie it, they can help to see how it fits in with other aspects of education. They also help to situate teachers' actions with their beliefs and reality. For many years constructivism has had a major influence on how we think about science teaching and learning (Duit & Treagust, 1998; Tobin, 1993). Constructivism as a learning theory has its origins in the work of Jean Piaget (1964) and Lev Vygotsky (1978). To Piaget, the learning of knowledge is constructed through an interaction of the learner's thoughts and prior experiences with others' ideas and experiences (Piaget, 1964). Vygotsky (1978) also conceived of learning as a constructivist process, but saw it as being mediated through social interactions. As a learning theory, constructivism concentrates on how individuals construct their world, believing that reality is co-constructed by the surrounding world (Sipe & Constable, 1996). From this idea of constructivism, science teachers who engage in collaborative action research have the opportunity to construct their understanding of their practice and their educational situation as they share and question one another's stories of practice.

Constructivism is also a way to understand how new knowledge is created. As such, it is a way of understanding what we mean by knowledge, science, and doing science (Feyerabend, 1975; Kuhn, 1996; Lakatos, 1978) and is a theory of knowledge (Bettencourt, 1993). For example, Ernst Von Glasersfeld (1993) wrote "constructivism deals with questions of knowledge – what knowledge is and where it comes from" (p. 23). As with constructivist learning theory, constructivist epistemology recognizes the construction of knowledge to be a social process, and is influenced by both the research community and the broader setting. Knowledge construction by science teachers engaged in action research is tied to, and explained by, a social system influenced by those surrounding them, such as their colleagues, administrators, parents, and students (Briscoe & Wells, 2002; Kemmis, 2009). It is by their interactions with the environment through communication, negotiation, and meaning-making they collectively develop knowledge. From this perspective, action research is a process in which practitioner knowledge is constructed through research.

The adjective "constructivist" has also been used to describe particular teaching methods. For the most part, all recent, reform-based advances in science teaching are based on constructivist learning theory and therefore can be labeled constructivist. These include the use of inquiry methods, the promotion of discussions, small group work, and the idea that students need to learn how to argue from evidence. From this perspective, the methods of action research can also be thought of as constructivist. Overall, as Lincoln (2001) noted, "while there are many links between action research and educators in the classroom, constructivism offers the most familiar and practical threads to bind the beliefs of educators and action researchers" (p. 130). From this, we can think of science teachers engaging in action research to be constructors of their own understanding of teaching practice and their educational situations; as constructors of new knowledge about science teaching and learning; and as taking part in constructivist methods.

As we've noted above, in action research, science teachers generate knowledge of practice rather than finding themselves as objects of research whose sole role is to implement the existing theory in practice (Peters, 2004). Thus, the purpose of action research is not to bring teachers' practices into conformity with existing educational theories, but to have them construct their own practical theories by inquiring into situations that are often contextually specific to their classroom environments and students' needs. Classrooms are socially mediated sites, and action research provides a greater understanding of self, and constructs new knowledge of how to negotiate these socially mediated environments. Thus, theory is embodied within and generated through teachers' practices and actions (Whitehead, 2000). These practical theories that result from action research are valuable because they are rooted in teachers' sense of self and practice, and they provide meaningful aspects of knowledge constructed from teachers' experiences in their daily work and interaction with students (Feldman et al., 2018). In this way, science teachers are practitioners, researchers, and theorists at the same time.

For example, Jawaher worked with a group of four high school science teachers from a large school district in the eastern region of Saudi Arabia. Their primary focus was the improvement of their ability to engage students in the practice of science in an online environment using digital game-based learning (DGBL) at the start of the COVID-19 pandemic (Alsultan, 2021a). The result of their action research led to the development of the Planning, Realization, and Assessment (PRA) framework of teachers' pedagogical roles and activities in the DGBL processes. In PRA, science teachers take on various roles. These include planner and organizer; facilitator of students learning science through playing games; and evaluator of students' learning. They are also self-evaluators of their integration of games, paying attention to the classroom environment and learning outcomes, such as the skills and knowledge students gain. Through this process the science teachers define how successful the innovations in their practice were, and what they should change in the future.

The PRA framework was developed by the science teachers who worked with Jawaher taking on all three aspects of constructivism. The origin of the framework was a systematic literature review done by Jawaher on how high school science teachers integrate digital games in classroom settings (Alsultan, 2021b). The teachers engaged as constructivist learners as they came to understand what Jawaher constructed from the literature. As the teachers engaged their students in DBGL, they revised the framework, which was a knowledge construction process. Their revision focused on how science teachers can integrate games as platforms for experimentation rather than content delivery systems. In this way, the use of the games enhanced students' conceptual scientific understanding, promoted their science inquiry-based learning, and developed their creativity, critical thinking, and problem-solving skills.

What is made clear by this example is that action research can be central to the growth of science teachers as inquirers in which they are developing principles and theories to guide their practice (Kemmis, 2009; Mills, 2018; Whitehead, 2000). It enables and supports teachers in pursuing effective pedagogical practices by transforming the quality of teaching decisions and actions to subsequently enhance student engagement and learning (Feldman et al., 2018; Kemmis, 2009). In short, action research is a process of self and practice transformation. This transformation happens as educators inquire about their practice and its underpinning assumptions that, in turn, enable them to develop a deep understanding of themselves and their own processes of learning and growth (McNiff, 2013).

Action Research in Science Education

In this section we turn specifically to action research in science education. We first examine a typology of modes of science teacher action research. We then look at how action research has been used to improve science teaching and learning.

Modes of Science Teacher Action Research

As we've noted several times already, there are multiple varieties of action research. Some ways to categorize them is by the roles teachers play (Eilks,

2013; Eilks & Markic, 2011; Feldman et al., 2022; Grundy, 1982; Laudonia et al., 2018), and the teachers' primary goals (Feldman et al., 2022; Laudonia et al., 2018). For example, Kemmis and his colleague Robin McTaggart (2005) described how action research can differ in the problems it addresses, settings, and involved individuals. This led to their typology of action research including participatory research, critical action research, classroom action research, action learning, action science, soft systems approach, and industrial action research. Similarly, Carr and Kemmis (1986) distinguished three action research models based on the theory of knowledge-constitutive interests proposed by Habermas (1971): technical action research focuses on improving control over outcomes, practical action research focuses on empowering practitioners, and critical action research focuses on justice.

A systematic review conducted by Ivano Laudonia and his colleagues (2018) resulted in a way to categorize action research in science education according to its purposes and modes. The purposes they identified were inquiring into students' cognition of science, the improvement of science curriculum, and the professional development of science teachers. These purposes would fit in Noffke's (1997) professional and personal purposes (see Chapter 8). Their modes of action research were technical, interactive, and teacher-centered. Feldman et al. (2022) expanded and modified this typology of modes to include participatory action research.

Technical Action Research.

According to Laudonia et al. (2018) technical action research is a facilitator-oriented approach where an outsider researcher takes the lead in the research process. The teachers' primary roles in this type of action research are to aid the researcher by offering a field of practice, conducting the intervention or experiment, and providing data and feedback (Eilks, 2018; Feldman et al., 2022; Laudonia et al., 2018). It is technical because the teachers act as technicians. Thus, in this type of action research, the relationship between the researcher and teacher takes a one-way approach that implies teachers are incapable of making decisions about their own practice (McNiff, 2013). In this way, technical action research focuses on outside researcher concerns instead of the teachers themselves (Feldman, 2017). Therefore, it is unsurprising that many scholars do not consider this technical mode a type of action research (Feldman et al., 2022). It is important to note, however, that others use "technical" to describe action research that focuses on straightforward problem solving, without necessarily having an outside facilitator. Primarily the main task in that type of technical action research is to improve the means of the practice to be more effective in assembling known ends, such as improving students' test scores in a class (Kemmis, 2009).

Laudonia et al. (2018) used a study published by Janice Koch and David Burghardt (2002) as an example of a science education technical action research project. The approach focused on enhancing and deepening students' conceptual understanding of science, mathematics, and technology education. Students were asked to develop solutions to technical problems using science, mathematics, and technical knowledge. During this process, the teachers were supported and helped by external researchers. Another example is one done by Asma Hawamdeh (2020) in Jordan. This study sought to improve 4th grade students' conceptual understanding of astronomy by implementing a role-playing strategy. The findings indicated the role-playing strategy positively helped develop students' interpretive skills by enhancing the understanding of astronomical phenomena, addressing conceptual misunderstandings, and pro-viding elements of pleasure and simulation in learning science. In both of these examples the science teachers served as assistants to the outside researchers, who were the authors of the studies.

Interactive Action Research

Interactive action research focuses on the mutual negotiation and cooperation between an outside researcher and teachers in identifying problems, developing the research methods, suggesting potential actions, and making decisions (Feldman et al., 2022; Laudonia et al., 2018). The external researcher can also take on the role of both co-researcher and co-teacher. This is also sometimes called collaborative action research.

To Wells (2009), interactive action research is a more powerful and bene-ficial method for other teachers than the technical method because it includes teachers' experiences and reflections about learning and teaching in their own classrooms. Similarly, Kemmis (2009) highlighted the uniqueness of interactive action research, writing, "the practitioner is the one who decides what is to be done, what is to be changed, and what sense is to be made of the observations made" (p. 469). However, to be effective and successful in improving the practice and generating knowledge the individuals involved in interactive action research must function as both a community of practice (Wenger, 1998) and an epistemic community (Créplet et al., 2003), or knowledge creating community. In order to meet these two conditions, teachers need to have a thorough foundation in the nature of action research and familiarity with the appropriate research methods (Capobianco & Feldman, 2006; 2010).

Mónica Borjas and Fátima De la Peña-Leyva (2009) carried out interactive action research with five secondary science teachers in Colombia (Feldman et al., 2022). In the project, teachers were involved in action research cycles starting with exploring different models for developing creative thinking. Then they worked collaboratively to select one model and develop their lessons based on the selected model. Finally, they reflected on their integration of this model. Borjas and De la Peña-Leyva (2009) studied the teachers' involvement in the action research through teacher focus groups, student interviews, class-room observations, and project meetings. They found that science teachers' active participation in designing the lessons and engagement in the action research process highly improved their practice. In this example, we can see the hallmark of interactive action research is the collaboration between the external researchers and the science teachers, who are internal to their practice situations, which appears in their negotiation about research focus, methods, data collection process, and future actions.

Teacher-Centered Action Research

Teacher-centered action research is a more self-directed and teacher-oriented type of action research (Kemmis, 2009; Mamlok-Naaman et al., 2005). This approach views science teachers as capable of conducting research and making decisions about their own practice (McNiff, 2013). Teachers develop their research by defining a problem in their practice, determining the method based on their investigations, identifying appropriate actions, collecting data, and deciding on practice changes. Thus, the objectives of teacher-centered action research are more beneficial because the focus is not just on the means of the practice but rather on changes and development of the practice (Kemmis, 2009).

Even though this model of action research is more independent, in some cases, outside researchers or experts may support and help the science teachers in conducting their classroom-based research, for example, training them in a specific research method or helping them find relevant literature (Feldman et al., 2022; Laudonia et al., 2018). The aid also can be provided from cooperation with a group of teachers who share the same goal and interest. The primary difference between teacher-centered and interactive modes is that the science teachers take the primary role in the research in the former, while in the latter, external researchers or colleagues take a consultative role (Feldman et al., 2018). Most of the examples of action research that we provide in Chapter 8 are of this mode. Therefore, we will not present any examples here.

Participatory Action Research

Participatory action research (PAR) was developed as a form of community-based research done by people who have been disenfranchised in some way. It is collaborative in nature and brings together ordinary people, many who have been marginalized in some way, to investigate and uncover power structures that define and limit their lives (Cammarota & Fine, 2010; Kemmis et al., 2013; Park, 2006; Puig et al., 2015; Susskind et al., 2018). Much PAR has had a literacy focus because of how illiteracy can result in disempowerment (Freire, 1970). It is also political in nature and is often guided by critical theories (Quicke, 1995), including feminist theory (van der Meulen, 2011), critical race theory (Torre, 2009), and Marxism (Fals-Borda, 1987).

PAR is not used by science teachers as much as the other modes of action research. We believe the primary reason for this is that science teachers do not see themselves as marginalized or disenfranchised. That said, there are powerful examples, including Brenda Capobianco's work with science teachers in

Massachusetts to explore feminist pedagogy (Capobianco, 2007; Capobianco et al., 2006); Renee Baynes' (2016) collaboration with science teachers in Australia to include Indigenous knowledges and perspectives in their classroom practice (see Chapter 8 for more information about Capobianco's and Baynes' studies); and the work that Chris Gayford (2001) did with secondary teachers in the UK to take charge of their professional development in order to determine how best to incorporate education for sustainability into their curricula.

Action Research for the Improvement of Science Teaching and Learning

The literature has many examples of action research for inquiring into students' cognition of science, science curriculum development and implementation, science teachers' professional development, and equity and social justice in science teaching and learning (Eilks, 2018; Feldman et al., 2022; Feldman & Capobianco, 2000; Laudonia et al., 2018).

Science Learning Outcomes

There is ample evidence in the literature stressing that action research is a valuable way for teachers to improve their practice so their students gain conceptual understanding of scientific principles (e.g., Baird & Mitchell, 1987; Fazio & Melville, 2008; Hawamdeh, 2020; Mitchell & Mitchell, 2008; Solomon et al., 1992; Whyte, 1986). A prime example was the work done by Jim Minstrell as he applied cognitive science learning principles in his own teaching of high school science. For more than 20 years, Minstrell investigated his teaching practice and students' learning of physics using audiotape, videotape, and interviews which led to methods for supporting students' development of a deep conceptual understanding of physics concepts (Feldman & Minstrell, 2000; Minstrell, 1992). The Project for Enhancing Effective Learning (PEEL) was a long-term action research project in Australia (Baird & Mitchell, 1987; Mitchell & Mitchell, 2008). It utilized collaborative action research among teachers and with university researchers to improve the teachers' practice for helping their students gain a conceptual understanding of science. In their book chapter Feldman et al. (2022) included an example from Malaysia in which Lilia Halim and her colleagues (2014) had the aim to help secondary students overcome their misconceptions about forces in equilibrium.

Science Curriculum Development

Action research has also been used to improve science curriculum at all levels from primary school (Koch & Burghardt, 2002; Solomon et al., 1992), to secondary school (Eilks, 2005; Eilks et al., 2010; Feldman, 1996; Lee &Yang, 2019; Marks & Eilks, 2010), to university (Gray et al., 2007). For example, Ingo Eilks and his colleagues led a five-year project in Germany that aimed to enrich the science curriculum by incorporating various cooperative learning methods into secondary school chemistry (Eilks, 2005; Eilks et al., 2010; Markic & Eilks, 2006; Witteck & Eilks, 2006). The result of the project illustrated changes in the teaching practices in which teachers implemented more cooperative and student-centered pedagogies. At the elementary level Karen Goodnough (2008) worked with a group of elementary teachers in Canada to help plan and implement a Problem-Based Learning (PBL) science curriculum.

Science Teachers' Professional Development

There are numerous examples of science teachers engaging in action research to improve their teaching practice, which has resulted in fundamental professional change and growth (Briscoe & Wells, 2002; Feldman et al., 2022; Mamlok-Naaman & Eilks, 2012). This includes the way they view themselves as professionals as well as how they envision student learning and their commitment to improving science teaching and learning (Alsultan, 2021a; Borjas & De la Peña-Leyva, 2009; Feldman et al., 2021; Gayford, 2001; Goodnough, 2010; Küçük & Çepni, 2005; Laudonia et al., 2018; Mamlok-Naaman, 2018; Megowan-Romanowicz, 2010). We provide several examples of this in Chapter 8.

Equity and Social Justice in Science Teaching and Learning

When action research is done to promote equity and social justice, science teachers are responding to the wicked educational problems they continuously face. Feldman et al. (2022) emphasized how teachers' engagement in action research for promoting social justice is beneficial in two ways:

> Although action research for equity and social justice focuses on serving the other – often students marginalized in science because of their race, ethnicity, first language, or immigrant status – it cannot be successful without science teachers learning new ways to reach the students, as well as changing their beliefs about who their students are as learners and human beings.
>
> (p. 359)

Many proponents of action research see it as an emancipatory process that can be used to uncover and transform inequities in schools (Carr & Kemmis, 1986; Fals-Borda, 1987; Feldman et al., 2015; Kemmis et al., 2013). For example, Mary Brenner and her colleagues (2016) investigated how the impact of science and mathematics teachers' engagement in the action research process informed and shaped their views related to three strands of equity: teachers and teaching, students and learning, and students' families and communities. They found most of the science teachers transformed their understanding of themselves and their students as a result of their action research. However, their views of families and communities changed in less substantive ways. In another study, Joyce Nyhof-Young (2000) looked at her role as convenor and facilitator of a group of five science teachers who delved into their own theories and practices in the context of gender issues in science education.

We end this section with an example from South Africa (de Beer, 2019). The focus of The Decolonisation of the Curriculum Project was to help science teachers transform their pedagogy and to infuse Indigenous knowledge into the curriculum. Phase 2 of the project, which took place in the Northern Cape, incorporated collaborative action research with 37 life science teachers. The pedagogical focus was the use of problem-based and project-based learning. Elsa Mentz and Josef de Beer (2019), who studied the effects of the teachers' action research, found many examples of effective incorporation of Indigenous knowledge into the regular science curriculum, as well as examples of the use of PBL in those units. It's interesting to note that the design of phase 2 was based on the researchers' study of their implementation of phase 1. In phase 1 they found the science teachers' curriculum work was not very reflective and did not adequately incorporate either the PBL or Indigenous knowledge. As a result, they decided to engage the teachers in action research for the phase 2 PD.

Summary

The primary goal of this chapter was to provide readers with foundational knowledge about action research in science education including models, characteristics, purpose, and theoretical and contextual points of view. As will be seen in the rest of this book, we support and promote modes that put science teachers in the forefront of their action research, and go beyond addressing straightforward, technical problems. This will become clear in the next chapter that sheds light on dialogic collaborative action research (D-CAR), its definition, purpose, and method, and discusses examples of implementing D-CAR in science education.

References

Alsultan, J. (2021a). *Saudi high school science teachers' perceptions towards the integration of digital game-based learning into their teaching practice.* Dissertation, University of South Florida, Tampa, FL.

Alsultan, J. (2021b). Pedagogical principles for advancing digital game-based learning in high school science education; a systematic review of selected empirical research from 2009 to 2019. Paper presented at the Society for Information Technology & Teacher Education International Conference, March 29 – April 2 [online].

Baird, J. R., & Mitchell, I. J. (eds.). (1987). *Improving the quality of teaching and learning: An Australian study case, the PEEL project.* Melbourne: The PEEL Group, Monash University.

Bassey, M. (1998). Action research for improving practice. In R. Halsall (ed.), *Teacher research and school improvement: Opening doors from the inside* (pp. 93–108). Buckingham, UK: Open University Press.

BAWP (1979). *Bay Area Writing Project/ California Writing Project/ National Writing Project: An overview.* Berkeley, CA: University of California.

Baynes, R. (2016). Teachers' attitudes to including Indigenous knowledges in the Australian science curriculum. *Australian Journal of Indigenous Education*, 45(1), 80–90. doi:10.1017/jie.2015.29.

Bettencourt, A. (1993). The construction of knowledge: A radical constructivist view. In K. Tobin (ed.), *The practice of constructivism in science education* (pp. 39–49). Washington, DC: American Association for the Advancement of Science Press.

Borjas, M. P., & De la Peña Leyva, F. (2009). Desarrollo de habilidades de pensamiento creativo en el área de Ciencias Naturales y Educación Ambiental. *Zona próxima*, no. 10, 12–35.

Brenner, M. E., Bianchini, J. A., & Dwyer, H. A. (2016). Science and mathematics teachers working toward equity through teacher research: Tracing changes across their research process and equity views. *Journal of Science Teacher Education*, 27(8), 819–845. doi:10.1007/s10972-016-9490-3.

Briscoe, C., & Wells, E. (2002). Reforming primary science assessment practices: A case study of one teacher's professional development through action research. *Science Education*, 86(3), 417–435. doi:200F;10.1002/sce.10021.

Buckingham, B. R. (1926). *Research for teachers.* New York: Silver, Burdette and Company.

Cammarota, J., & Fine, M. (2010). Youth participatory action research: A pedagogy for transformational resistance. In J. Cammarota & M. Fine (eds.), *Revolutionizing education: Youth participatory action research in motion* (pp. 9–20). New York: Routledge.

Capobianco, B. M. (2007). Science teachers' attempts at integrating feminist pedagogy through collaborative action research. *Journal of Research in Science Teaching*, 44(1), 1–32. doi:10.1002/tea.20120.

Capobianco, B. M., & Feldman, A. (2006). Promoting quality for teacher action research: Lessons learned from science teachers' action research. *Educational Action Research*, 14(4), 497–512. doi:10.1080/09650790600975668.

Capobianco, B. M., & Feldman, A. (2010). Repositioning teacher action research in science teacher education. *Journal of Science Teacher Education*, 21(8), 909–915. doi:10.1007/s10972-010-9219-7.

Capobianco, B. M., Lincoln, S., Canuel-Browne, D., & Trimarchi, R. (2006). Examining the experiences of three generations of teacher researchers through collaborative science teacher inquiry. *Teacher Education Quarterly* (Summer), 61–78.

Carr, W., & Kemmis, S. (1986). *Becoming critical: Education, knowledge and action research.* London: Falmer Press.

Clift, R., Veal, M. L., Johnson, M., & Holland, P. (1990). Restructuring teacher education through collaborative action research. *Journal of Teacher Education*, 41(2), 52–62. doi:10.1177/00224871900410020.

Corey, S. M. (1949). Curriculum development through action research. *Educational Leadership*, 7(3), 147–153.

Corey, S. M. (1953). *Action research to improve school practices.* New York: Teachers College Press.

Créplet, F., Dupouet, O. & Vaast, E. (2003). Episteme or practice? Differentiated communitarian structures in a biology laboratory In M. Huysman, E. Wenger, & V. Wulf (eds), *Communities and technologies* (pp. 43–63). Dordrecht: Kluwer Academic Publishers.

de Beer, J. (ed.). (2019). *The decolonisation of the curriculum project: The affordances of indigenous knowledge for self-directed learning*, NWU Self-directed Learning Series. Capetown: AOSIS. doi:0.4102/aosis.2019.BK133.

Dewey, J. (1929). *The sources of a science of education*, vol. 17. New York: Horace Liveright.

Duit, R., & Treagust, D. F. (1998). Learning in science – from behaviorism towards social constructivism and beyond. In B. J. Fraser & K. Tobin (eds.), *International handbook of science education* (pp. 3–25). Dordrecht: Kluwer.

Eilks, I. (2005). Experiences and reflections about teaching atomic structure in a jigsaw classroom in lower secondary school chemistry lessons. *Journal of Chemical Education*, 82, 313–320.

Eilks, I. (2013). Action research in science education: From general justifications to a specific model in practice. In T. Stern, F. Rauch, A. Schuster, & A. Townsend (eds.), *Action research, innovation and change* (pp. 172–192). London: Routledge.

Eilks, I. (2018). Action research in science education: A twenty-year personal perspective. *Action Research and Innovation in Science Education*, 1(1), 3–14. doi:10.51724/arise.5.

Eilks, I., & Markic, S. (2011). Effects of a long-term participatory action research project on science teachers' professional development. *Eurasia Journal of Mathematics, Science and Technology Education*, 7(3), 149–160. doi:10.12973/ejmste/75196.

Eilks, I., Markic, S., & Witteck, T. (2010). Collaborative innovation of the science classroom by participatory action research – theory and practice in a project of implementing cooperative learning methods in chemistry education. In M. Valenčič Zuljan & J. Vogrinc (eds.), *Facilitating effective student learning through teacher research and innovation* (pp. 77–101). Ljubljana: University of Ljubljana.

Elliott, J. (1991). *Action research for educational change*. Philadelphia, PA: Open University Press.

Fals-Borda, O. (1987). The application of participatory action-research in Latin America. *International Sociology*, 2(4), 329–347. doi:10.1177/026858098700200401.

Fazio, X., & Melville, W. (2008). Science teacher development through collaborative action research. *Teacher Development*, 12(3), 193–209. doi:10.1080/13664530802259222.

Feldman, A. (1996). Enhancing the practice of physics teachers: Mechanisms for the generation and sharing of knowledge and understanding in collaborative action research. *Journal of Research in Science Teaching*, 33(5), 513–540. doi:doi:10.1002/(SICI)1098-2736(199605)33:5<513::AID-TEA4>3.0.CO;2-U.

Feldman, A. (2017). An emergent history of educational action research in the English-speaking world. In L. L. Rowell, C. D. Bruce, J. M. Shosh, & M. M. Riel (eds.), *The Palgrave international handbook of action research* (pp. 125–145). New York: Palgrave Macmillan.

Feldman, A., & Capobianco, B. (2000). *Action research in science education*. ERIC Digest.

Feldman, A., & Minstrell, J. (2000). *Action research as a research methodology for the study of the teaching and learning of science*. ERIC Clearinghouse. https://people.umass.edu/~afeldman/ActionResearchPapers/FeldmanMinstrell2000.PDF.

Feldman, A., Altrichter, H., Posch, P., & Somekh, B. (2018). *Teachers investigate their work: An introduction to action research across the professions* (3rd edition). New York: Routledge.

Feldman, A., Belova, N., Eilks, I., Kapanadze, M., Mamlok-Naaman, R., Rauch, F., & Taşar, M. F. (2022). Action research: A promising strategy for science teacher education. In J. A. Luft & M. G. Jones (eds.), *Handbook of research on science teacher education* (pp. 352–362). New York: Routledge.

Feldman, A., Bennett, K., & Vernaza-Hernández, V. (2015). Responsible action research for the pursuit of justice. *Educational Action Research*, 23(1), 85–103. doi:10.1080/09650792.2014.994014.

Feldman, A., Nation, M., & Laux, K. (2021). The effects of extended action research-based professional development on the teaching of climate science. *Educational Action Research*, 1–17. doi:10.1080/09650792.2021.1981417.

Feyerabend, P. (1975). *Against method: Outline of an anarchistic theory of knowledge.* London and New York: Verso Press.

Foshay, A. W. (1994). Action research: An early history in the United States. *Journal of Curriculum and Supervision*, 9(4), 317–325.

Freire, P. (1970). *Pedagogy of the oppressed.* New York: Continuum.

Gayford, C. (2001). Education for sustainability: An approach to the professional development of teachers. *European Journal of Teacher Education*, 24(3), 313–327. doi:10.1080/02619760220128879.

Goodnough, K. (2008). Examining the personal side of change within a collaborative inquiry group: Adopting Problem-Based Learning in primary/elementary science education. *Journal of Applied Research on Learning*, 2(1), 1–23.

Goodnough, K. (2010). Teacher learning and collaborative action research: Generating a "knowledge-of-practice" in the context of science education. *Journal of Science Teacher Education*, 21, 917–935.

Gray, K., Chang, R., & Radloff, A. (2007). Enhancing the scholarship of teaching and learning: Evaluation of a scheme to improve teaching and learning through action research. *International Journal of Teaching and Learning in Higher Education*, 19(1), 21–32.

Green, J., & Dixon, C. (1993). Talking knowledge into being: Discursive and social practices in classrooms. *Linguistics and Education*, 5(3–4), 231–239.

Grundy, S. (1982). Three modes of action research. *Curriculum Perspectives*, 2(3), 23–34.

Habermas, J. (1971). *Knowledge and Human Interests*, translated by J. J. Shapiro. London: Polity Press.

Halim, L., Yong, T. K., & Meerah, T. S. M. (2014). Overcoming students' misconceptions on forces in equilibrium: An action research study. *Creative Education*, 5(11).

Hawamdeh, A. A. (2020). How does the role-playing strategy affect the development of interpretive skills for astronomical phenomena among fourth-grade female students? *Action Research and Innovation in Science Education*, 3(2), 39–42. doi:10.12973/arise/295514.

Hendricks, C. C. (2019). History of action research in education. In C. A. Mertler (ed.), *The Wiley handbook of action research in education* (pp. 29–52). New York: John Wiley & Sons, Inc.

Kemmis, S. (2009). Action research as a practice-based practice. *Educational Action Research*, 17(3), 463–474. doi:10.1080/09650790903093284.

Kemmis, S., & McTaggart, R. (2005). Participatory action research: Communicative action and the public sphere. In N. Denzin & Y. Lincoln (eds.), *Handbook of qualitative research* (pp. 556–604). Thousand Oaks, CA: Sage.

Kemmis, S., McTaggart, R., & Nixon, R. (2014). *The action research planner: Doing critical participatory action research.* New York: Springer.

Kemmis, S., & McTaggart, R. (1986). *The action research planner* (3rd edition). Geelong, Australia: Deakin University Press.

Koch, J., & Burghardt, M. D. (2002). Design technology in the elementary school: A study of teacher action research. *Journal of Technology Education*, 13(2), 21–33.

Koshy, V. (2009). *Action research for improving educational practice: A step-by-step guide*. London and Thousand Oaks, CA: Sage Publications.

Küçük, M., & Çepni, S. (2005). Implementation of an action research course program for science teachers: A case for Turkey. *The Qualitative Report*, 10(2), 190–207.

Kuhn, T. S. (1996). *The structure of scientific revolutions* (vol. 2). Chicago, IL: University of Chicago Press.

Lakatos, I. (1978). *The methodology of scientific research programmes*. Cambridge: Cambridge University Press.

Laudonia, I., Mamlok-Naaman, R., Abels, S., & Eilks, I. (2018). Action research in science education – an analytical review of the literature. *Educational Action Research*, 26(3), 480–495. doi:10.1080/09650792.2017.1358198.

Laux, K. (2019). *Changing high school science teacher beliefs on student voice through action research* (Publication Number 13903130). PhD, University of South Florida. ProQuest Dissertations & Theses Global, Ann Arbor, MI.

Lee, H., & Yang, J.-e. (2019). Science teachers taking their first steps toward teaching sociocentric issues through collaborative action research. *Research in Science Education*, 49(1), 51–71. doi:10.1007/s11165–11017–9614–9616.

Lewin, K. (1946). Action research and minority problems. *Journal of Social Issues*, 2(4), 34–46.

Lincoln, Y. S. (2001). Engaging sympathies: Relationships between action research and social constructivism. In P. Reason & H. Bradbury (eds.), *Handbook of action research: Participative inquiry and practice* (pp. 124–132). Thousand Oaks, CA: Sage Publications.

Loughran, J. (1996). *Developing reflective practice: Learning about teaching and learning through modeling*. London: Falmer Press.

Mamlok-Naaman, R. (2018). Using the action research rationale to enhance the creation of teachers' professional learning communities (PLCs). *Action Research and Innovation in Science Education*, 1(1), 27–32.

Mamlok-Naaman, R., & Eilks, I. (2012). Different types of action research to promote chemistry teachers' professional development – a joined theoretical reflection on two cases from Israel and Germany. *International Journal of Science and Mathematics Education*, 10(3), 581–610. doi:10.1007/s10763-011-9306-z.

Mamlok-Naaman, R., Navon, O., Carmeli, M., & Hofstein, A. (2005). Chemistry teachers research their own work two case studies. In K. M. Boersma, O. De Jong, & H. Eijkelhof (eds.), *Research and the quality of science education* (pp. 141–156). Heidelberg: Springer. doi:10.1007/1-4020-3673-6_12.

Markic, S., & Eilks, I. (2006). Cooperative and context-based learning on electrochemical cells in lower secondary chemistry: A project of participatory action research. *Science Education International*, 17(4), 253–273.

Marks, R., & Eilks, I. (2010). Research-based development of a lesson plan on shower gels and musk fragrances following a socio-critical and problem-oriented approach to chemistry teaching. *Chemistry Education: Research and Practice*, 11, 129–141.

McDonagh, C., Roche, M., Sullivan, B., & Glenn, M. (2020). *Enhancing practice through classroom research: A teacher's guide to professional development*. New York: Routledge.

McNiff, J. (2013). *Action research: Principles and practice.* New York: Routledge.

McTaggart, R. (1991). *A short modern history.* Geelong, Australia: Deakin University Press.

Megowan-Romanowicz, C. (2010). Inside out: Action research from the teacher–researcher perspective. *Journal of Science Teacher Education,* 21(8), 993–1011. doi:10.1007/s10972-010-9214-z.

Mentz, E., & de Beer, J. (2019). The use of Cultural-Historical Activity Theory in researching the affordances of indigenous knowledge for self-directed learning. In J. de Beer (ed.), *The decolonisation of the curriculum project: The affordances of indigenous knowledge for self-directed learning* (Vol. NWU Self-directed Learning Series, pp. 49–86). Capetown: AOSIS. doi:10.4102/aosis.2019.BK133.03.

Mills, G. E. (2018). *Action research: A guide for the teacher researcher* (6th edition). London: Pearson.

Minstrell, J. (1992). Facets of students' knowledge and relevant instruction. In R. Duit, F. Goldberg, & H. Niedderer (eds.), *Research in physics learning: Theoretical issues and empirical studies* (pp. 110–128). Hamburg: Kiel.

Mitchell, I., & Mitchell, J. (2008). The Project for Enhancing Effective Learning (PEEL): 22 years of praxis. In A. P. Samaras, A. R. Freese, C. Kosnik, & C. Beck (eds.), *Learning communities in practice* (pp. 7–18). Springer Netherlands. doi:10.1007/978-1-4020-8788-2_1.

Mitchell, S. N., Reilly, R. C., & Logue, M. E. (2009). Benefits of collaborative action research for the beginning teacher. *Teaching and Teacher Education,* 25(2), 344–349. doi:10.1016/j.tate.2008.06.008.

Noffke, S. E. (1990). *Action research: A multidimensional analysis.* Madison, WI: The University of Wisconsin-Madison.

Noffke, S. E. (1997). Professional, personal, and political dimensions of action research. *Review of Research in Education,* 22, 305–343. doi:10.3102/0091732X022001305.

Nyhof-Young, J. (2000). The political is personal: Reflections on facilitating action research in gender issues in science education. *Educational Action Research,* 8(3), 471–498. doi:10.1080/09650790000200134.

Park, P. (2006). Knowledge and participatory research. In P. Reason & H. Bradbury (eds.), *Handbook of action research: Concise paperback edition* (pp. 83–93). Sage Publications.

Peters, J. (2004). Teachers engaging in action research: challenging some assumptions. *Educational Action Research,* 12(4), 535–556. doi:10.1080/09650790400200267.

Piaget, J. (1964). Development and learning. *Journal of Research in Science Teaching,* 2, 176–186.

Puig, V. I., Erwin, E. J., Evenson, T. L., & Beresford, M. (2015). "It's a two-way street": Examining how trust, diversity, and contradiction influence a sense of community. *Journal of Research in Childhood Education,* 29(2), 187–201.

Quicke, J. (1995). Democracy and bureaucracy: Towards an understanding of the politics of educational action research. *Educational Action Research,* 3(1), 75–91. doi:10.1080/0965079950030107.

Sipe, L. & Constable, S. (1996). A chart of four contemporary research paradigms: Metaphors for the modes of inquiry. *TABOO: The Journal of Culture and Education,* 1, 153–163.

Solomon, J., Duveen, J., & Scot, L. (1992). Teaching about the nature of science through inquiry: Action research in the classroom. *Journal of Research in Science Teaching,* 29(4), 409–421.

Stenhouse, L. (1975). *An introduction to curriculum research and development.* London: Heinemann.

Stenhouse, L. (1981). What counts as research? *British Journal of Educational Studies,* 29(2), 103–114.

Susskind, L., Cunningham, D., & Cruxên, I. A. (2018). Teaching participatory action research: The search for pedagogical insights. In J. Calder & J. Foletta (eds.), *(Participatory) action research: Principles, approaches and applications* (pp. 125–150). Hauppauge, NY: Nova Science Publishers, Inc.

Tobin, K. G. (ed.). (1993). *The practice of constructivism in science education.* Washington, DC: AAAS Press.

Torre, M. E. (2009). Participatory action research and critical race theory: Fueling spaces for nos-otras to research. *The Urban Review,* 41(1), 106–120. doi:10.1007/s11256-008-0097-7.

van der Meulen, E. (2011). Action research with sex workers: Dismantling barriers and building bridges. *Action Research,* 9(4), 370–384. doi:10.1177/1476750311409767.

Von Glasersfeld, E. (1993). Questions and answers about radical constructivism. In K. G. Tobin (ed.), *The practice of constructivism in science education* (pp. 23–38). Washington, DC: American Association for the Advancement of Science Press.

Vygotsky, L. S. (1978). *Mind in society: The development of higher psychological processes.* Cambridge, MA: Harvard University Press.

Wells, G. (2009). Dialogic inquiry as collaborative action research. In S. E. Noffke & B. Somekh (eds.), *The Sage handbook of educational action research* (pp. 50–61). Sage.

Wenger, E. (1998). Communities of practice: Learning as a social system. *Systems Thinker,* 9(5), 1–10.

Whitehead, J. (2000). How do I improve my practice? Creating and legitimating an epistemology of practice. *Reflective Practice,* 1(1), 91–104. doi:10.1080/713693129.

Whyte, J. B. (1986). Starting early: Girls and engineering. *European Journal of Engineering Education,* 11(3), 271–279.

Witteck, T., & Eilks, I. (2006). Max Sour Ltd.– open experimentation and problem-solving in a cooperative learning company. *School Science Review,* 88(323), 95–102.

Zeichner, K. M., & Noffke, S. E. (2001). Practitioner research. In V. Richardson (ed.), *Handbook of research on teaching* (pp. 298–332). Washington, DC: American Educational Research Association.

3 Introduction to Dialogic Collaborative Action Research (D-CAR)

Introduction

In the preceding chapter we provided some background about the history and nature of action research, and its use in science education. We now turn to the focus of this book, dialogic collaborative action research (D-CAR), which relies on the power of conversations among small groups of teachers, in this case science teachers. We focus on D-CAR because of two primary reasons. The first is that from our experience, and our conversations with others who promote action research as a powerful tool for the improvement of science teaching and learning, science teachers rarely engage in conventional forms of action research as a regular part of their practice. While science teachers will, can, and do so when enrolled in courses or as part of funded projects, they stop engaging in the formal collection and analysis of data that is laid out as action research in most books about how to do it (for example see Feldman et al., 2018; McNiff, 2017; Mertler, 2019; Mills, 2018; Sagor & Williams, 2017). Therefore, we believe and have seen that a model like D-CAR is more doable given the constraints of teachers' work, and fits better into the time flow and rhythm of science teachers' daily practice. The second reason is that we believe science teachers face wicked problems in their work (see Chapter 4 for more information about wicked problems). These problems have to do with the nature of our contemporary society, and the concerns science teachers have for finding the best ways to reach and educate *all* of their students. Action research can be the tool through which science teachers move toward reaching the goal to address social justice and prepare citizens who have the knowledge and skills to engage with issues such as climate change and pandemics, but for that to happen, action research needs to be embedded into teachers' lives and work.

Collaboration

In the introduction to this chapter we described D-CAR as powerful conversations among small groups of science teachers. When science teachers engage in conversations, they are "working together towards the same end,

DOI: 10.4324/9781003307174-3

purpose, or effect" (Oxford Dictionaries, 2021), which is what it means to collaborate (from the Latin for work together). The idea of collaboration among teachers, or teachers with university researchers, stretches back over 40 years. For example, William Tikunoff and his colleagues in their final report of the Interactive Research and Development on Teaching project, wrote:

> collaboration is viewed as teachers, researchers, and trainer developers *working with parity* and *assuming equal responsibility* to identify, inquire into and resolve the problems and concerns of classroom teachers. Such collaboration recognizes and utilizes the insights and skills provided by each participant while, at the same time, demanding that no set of responsibilities is assigned a superior status.
>
> (Tikunoff et al., 1979, p. 10, emphasis in original)

It can be seen here that Tikunoff et al. (1979) provide a view of collaboration that stresses equity and discourages hierarchical relationships. However, collaboration at that time was often seen as a way for teachers to help university researchers study teaching. In a later publication, Tikunoff and Ward (1983) describe three outcomes of these collaborations: 1) they see a greater likelihood that the research findings will be used by teachers; 2) the research will more likely reflect the complexities of educational situations; and 3) it reduces the time between when the research project begins and when it is used in the classroom. That is, by involving teachers collaboratively with university researchers, it would reduce the theory/practice gap (Dewey, 1904; Korthagen, 2007). Ann Lieberman (1986) expanded this list to include encouraging collegiality among teachers, providing opportunities for teachers to be in leadership positions, and helping legitimize teachers' practical knowledge.

The legitimization of teachers' knowledge is also discussed in a recent article by Clive Dimmock (2016). In it, he presents an argument for schools to be what he describes as "research engaged," which is similar to the professional development school model developed in the 1990s (Darling-Hammond, 1994). An important aspect of Dimmock's model is collaboration between university researchers and teachers, as well as collaboration among teachers in professional learning communities (PLCs). Collaborations between university researchers and teachers are often focused on the formers' research interests rather than on the needs and concerns of teachers (Feldman, 1993), resulting in the "hijacking" of the teachers' research (Bevins & Price, 2014; Elliott, 1991). In the US, PLCs have become almost ubiquitous in schools (see for example, Stoll et al., 2006). However, they are often used by school administrators as time for teachers to complete administrative tasks rather than as a site for teacher inquiry and professional learning. Therefore, neither of these models of collaboration – the university researcher-dominated model with teachers or the task-oriented PLC – lead to the legitimization of teachers' knowledge or to their sense of professionalism.

A review of the literature on collaboration among teachers defined it as a "joint interaction in the group in all activities that are needed to perform a shared task" (Vangrieken et al., 2015, p. 23). However, Katrien Vangrieken and her colleagues note collaboration is a fluid term that has different meanings in different situations. Collaborative groups can have a variety of structures, such as within schools or across schools, or grade-level specific versus subject-specific. They can also be relatively permanent or ad hoc; or settled in its participant make-up or fluid in how they are constituted. Vangrieken et al. (2015) distinguish between the depth of the collaboration:

> These range from preserving individualism – focusing on individual teacher responsibility and autonomy, over coordination – coordinating responsibilities and tasks without discussion of the substance of teaching, cooperation – establishment of a common ground for joint enterprise through focusing on the content and process of classroom activity, and finally sharing – sharing and clarification of pedagogical motives that direct the way the teaching and learning is being structured.
>
> (Vangrieken et al., 2015, p. 26)

In D-CAR, collaboration goes beyond the individual to cooperation and sharing with a group.

Collaborative Action Research

As we noted in Chapter 2, action research can serve as a way for science teachers to collaborate with one another to improve their practice, share their practical theories, and construct new knowledge (Clift et al., 1990; Feldman et al., 2018; Mitchell et al., 2009). When action research is done as a collaborative activity among a group of teachers, the group takes on the characteristics of a professional community. Feldman et al. (2018) provide four advantages of teachers collaborating in groups as they engage in action research. First, a collaborative group provides a context in which the teachers can discuss the design, methods, and results of their research. Second, the group can develop into a collegial, professional community that focuses on the teachers' needs and concerns. Third, the group acts as a scientific community in which research results and warrants for them are shared and have to stand the test of critical discussion. Finally, as Stenhouse (1975, 1981) argued, research must be made public if it is to count as research. By sharing within the group, it becomes, at least on the local level, a mechanism for sharing the practical knowledge and theories uncovered and generated through the action research.

Although collaboration among teachers is an essential component of D-CAR, university researchers or school administrators can play important roles as facilitators of science teachers' action research groups or as critical friends (Blake & Gibson, 2021), and help develop each of the advantages we just discussed. That said, it is important for us to make clear at this point the focus of this book is on teachers working, learning, and researching together in ways that put their concerns in the forefront.

When science teachers collaborate with one another to engage in action research, their groups often have the characteristics of a community of practice. Etienne and Beverly Wenger-Traynor (2015) define communities of practice as "sustained learning partnerships among people who share a concern or a passion for something they do and learn how to do it better as they interact regularly" (p. 1). For a group to be a community of practice, it must have three main characteristics: the domain, the community, and the practice. The domain is the interest shared by members of the group. For the group to be a community, the members of the group "build relationships that enable them to learn from each other; they care about their standing with each other" (p.1). To have a practice means that the group members are practitioners. Because of this, as they engage with one another they "develop a shared repertoire of resources: experiences, stories, tools, ways of addressing recurring problems" (p. 3).

For a group consisting of teachers across grade levels and subjects, the domain could be as broad as the improvement of teaching. For science teachers, who are the focus of this book, the domain would relate in some way to the teaching and learning of science. For example, two of us worked with a group of high school science teachers whose primary focus of interest was the improvement of their ability to engage students in an online environment at the start of the COVID-19 pandemic (Feldman & Alsultan, 2022). We called the group the COVID Community of Practice. The practice shared by the group was the teaching of science at the high school level. The domain of the group was defined in part by characteristics shared by the teachers, including the practice of teaching science at the high school level, teaching in the same school district,[1] and the strong interest to find ways to engage their students in inquiry, discussion, and argumentation (IDA) in an online environment. As they engaged with each over during the project, the group acquired the characteristics of a community as they came to respect one another and develop the trust needed to share stories of practice.

In a community of practice the "members engage in joint activities and discussions, help each other, and share information" (Wenger-Trayner & Wenger-Trayner, 2015, p. 2). In doing so, they "build relationships that enable them to learn from each other; they care about their standing with each other" (Wenger-Trayner & Wenger-Trayner, 2015, p. 2). By the end of the six-week project described above, the teachers had developed collegial relationships, and in at least one case, a new friendship developed. It was also clear from evidence gathered by us, that the teachers had developed a strong sense of trust amongst themselves and with us (Feldman & Alsultan, 2022).

Members of communities of practice have a common professional practice. In our example, the members were engaged in the practice of teaching science. This community of practice developed a "shared repertoire of resources: experiences, stories, tools, ways of addressing recurring problems" (Wenger-

Trayner & Wenger-Trayner, 2015, p. 2) that built on their experiences of teaching high school science in the same school district, and responding to the challenge of suddenly teaching in an online environment.

The Nature of Dialogue

In the mid-1990s, Allan began to recognize the power of conversation as a research method. He first presented his thoughts at a conference in 1994 (Feldman, 1994) and subsequently published two papers on the role of conversation. The first was focused on the way he incorporated conversation into his teaching of action research (Feldman, 1998), and the second was an essay on the nature of conversation in collaborative action research (Feldman, 1999). Although Allan had talked and written about oral exchanges among people as conversations, his use of the term is synonymous with how other authors, and this book, use the term dialogue.

Allan began "The Role of Conversation in Collaborative Action Research" (1999) with three examples of D-CAR. The first was what Marilyn Cochran-Smith and Susan Lytle (1993) refer to as oral inquiry processes. They define oral inquiry processes as "procedures in which two or more teachers jointly research their experiences by examining particular issues, educational concepts, texts (including students' work), and other data about students" (p. 30). By definition, the processes are both collaborative and oral. By talking with one another about their practice and referring to classroom data, teachers build on each other's insights for problem posing and solving. The second example was what Sandra Hollingsworth (1994) described as collaborative conversations. In her analysis of the action research group that she worked with for several years, she saw how the collaborative conversations went beyond everyday talk to become a way for the teachers to research their practice so that transformative processes could occur. The final example was the Physics Teachers Action Research Group (PTARG). Allan's study of this group of teachers who were engaged in collaborative action research led to his uncovering of the model of enhanced normal practice (ENP), which we describe below.

In his paper (Feldman, 1999), Allan used the following characteristics to distinguish conversation (dialogue) from everyday talk: it is a cooperative activity; it has direction; and it results in new understanding. Understanding grows through the back-and-forth negotiations between the speaker and those who are listening, and between what was said and is being said. Those in dialogue make use of facts and assumptions, their experiences, and other features of their personal and educational situations. Nimrod Aloni describes this as a debate or exchange of ideas "that involves attentive listening and a sense of challenging, as well as inviting joint thought and a mutually beneficial exchange of ideas" (Aloni, 2013, p. 1072).

As a collaborative activity, the participants in the dialogue need to be cooperative with one another. That means it ought to take a "non-hierarchical approach and [embrace] a spirit of democracy, reciprocity and solidarity...

respect for the other by virtue of his or her humanity" (Aloni, 2013, p. 1072). An important aspect of dialogue is that it has direction, which arises from the dialogue itself and the new understandings that develop among the participants. To Aloni (2013), this means an aim towards mutual enrichment, inspiration, and transformation. They also have an intentional quality, which means they are related to something other than or beyond the conversation itself.

Carl Bereiter (1994) uses the term "progressive" to describe dialogue that generates a new understanding for participants that they see as being better than their previous understanding. For this to happen Bereiter argues the participants must make the following commitments:

- to work toward a common understanding that is satisfactory to all;
- to frame questions and statements of knowledge or understanding in ways that can be tested by evidence;
- to develop more statements of knowledge or understanding for which there is consensus among the participants;
- to allow any belief to be subjected to criticism if it will advance the discourse.

The new understandings that arise out of dialogues in collaborative action research can be transformed into knowledge as they are articulated and shared with others. The collaborative action research group then becomes a knowledge building, or epistemic, community (Créplet et al., 2003; Knorr Cetina, 1999).

Before we turn to the nature of D-CAR, we believe it is important to touch upon the genre of speech that can be used among participants in collaborative groups. There are those who have argued that teachers need to know and use specialized language to participate in knowledge building activities. We agree with the argument made by Ilana Horn and Britnie Kane (2019) that language arising as part of the common sense of teaching is sufficient for dialogues that can produce new knowledge or understanding. They refer to this as "professionalizing discourses" that allow teachers to delve into their existing conceptions, honor the highly contextualized nature of teaching, and enable them to consider the interrelationships that abound in classroom settings. In short, teachers can draw upon the language they usually use in their practice to describe and inquire into the many aspects of their work.

Dialogic Collaborative Action Research (D-CAR)

In Chapter 2, we provided an overview of the different ways that action research has been conceptualized and implemented. This is reflected in the many books for teachers on how to engage in action research (e.g., Feldman et al., 2018; McDonagh et al., 2020; McNiff, 2013; Mills, 2018). These books describe the methods of action research as a cycle that begins with reflection by the teachers on their educational situations to uncover any problems, dilemmas, or dissonances in their practice they feel are important for them to address. Sometimes the model begins with a period of reconnaissance to collect information on which to reflect (Elliott, 1991; Lewin, 1946). The teachers then plan and make changes in their practice based on those reflections. When they enact the changes, they can collect information about the implementation and collect other data on its impact. The teachers use this information to revise their action plans and take new actions. This cycle is repeated until the teachers have solved their problem, resolved their dilemma or dissonance, or are satisfied with the results of their action research. The gathering of information and reflection on it are usually described in action research books in ways parallel to the methods of research in the social sciences. We label this type of action research as conventional to indicate that this way of doing action research follows a set of conventions, which are similar to those used in research in the social sciences.

D-CAR differs from conventional forms of action research by putting the importance of conversation or dialogue amongst the group's members in the forefront. In D-CAR, conversation is the primary means by which the group members construct and share knowledge. That is because it is based on the idea that knowledge and understanding can be constructed when people engage in dialogue with one another (Feldman, 1998; Wells, 1999). The conversations in D-CAR are different from informal ones or chit-chat because they have a direction or intent (Feldman, 1999). In addition, because the D-CAR groups are communities of practice, the teachers share a common domain of interest and the desire to improve their practice. The conversations in D-CAR can lead to the outcomes of action research such as bringing to light new thoughts and ideas, improving communication among the teachers, and providing them with the knowledge and skills needed to make defensible decisions about goals and actions. In these types of conversations, as Wells (1999) noted, knowledge and understanding are created and shared among the group.

The use of dialogue or conversation in action research has been explored previously by others (e.g., Clark, 2001; Gordon, 1986; Hollingsworth, 1994; Kristiansen & Bloch-Poulsen, 2004; Laidlaw, 1994; Lowe et al., 2021; Pugach & Johnson, 1990); however, it has rarely been described as a method for doing research. We believe it is important to champion dialogical forms of action research because it reduces or eliminates the barriers teachers face when attempting to engage in conventional action research (see Chapter 7), and builds on what many science teachers already do.

In general, science teachers, whether inservice or preservice, engage in conventional action research because they are enrolled in a degree program that requires them to do so or they are part of a project that pays them to do so. There is also a possibility that action research is a requirement of their teaching job. However, this is actually quite rare. When science teachers don't have strong intrinsic reasons for doing conventional action research, the structure of teachers' work often leads to them abandoning its rigors when the incentives end (Feldman et al., 2001). Conventional action research requires a major time commitment by teachers and a significant increase to their workload because of the use of research methods similar to those used in the social sciences. It takes time to collect and analyze data, and to reach conclusions about how to make changes in teaching methods based on that analysis. As Stenhouse noted "The most serious impediment to the development of teachers as researchers ... is quite simply a shortage of time" (Stenhouse, 1981, p. 111). Even if they have the time to engage in conventional action research, there is also the issue that science teachers need the results of their action research sooner rather than later so they can incorporate these results in their ongoing practice. This results in conventional action research not meeting the day-to-day needs of teachers (Feldman & Atkin, 1995). Some may argue that to produce generalizable findings, the methods of conventional action research are needed. We respond by noting that science teachers are not so concerned with the results of their action research being applicable as widely as possible. Instead, their concern is with the immediate understanding of what works in their situations, and to be able to make use of it in the day-to-day flow of their practice. The understanding science teachers develop through D-CAR can be shared with other teachers, who could then use it without delay to better understand their practice, and modify it to improve their teaching and their students' learning.

Additionally, rather than being an add-on like conventional action research, D-CAR can be embedded in science teachers' work as an enhancement of the normal, everyday practice of good teachers. We think of "good teachers" as those who pay attention to their teaching and their students' learning, reflect on their observations, and then make changes in their practice based on their reflections. This idea of reflective practice was first introduced by Donald Schön (1983, 1987) and expanded on by many others (e.g., Jay & Johnson, 2002; Zeichner & Liston, 2014). D-CAR enhances the good science teacher's reflective practice in two ways. One is that it is done collaboratively among science teachers. They interact with one another as they focus on a common problem, or help each other as each focuses on a problem particular to their educational situations. The other is that conversation is the primary research mode. However, as we noted above, the conversation needs to have structure and be systematic, rather than informal chatter. This could be achieved by teachers agreeing on a set of norms and processes to structure their conversations, which we describe in Chapter 5. In the group meetings the conversations are systematic because the science teachers are part of a community of practice with its shared domain, community, and practice. In the group of high school science teachers we referred to above, they also shared concerns about larger educational issues, such as inequities related to student demographics and unequal distribution of resources. As the science teachers converse with each other, sharing concerns, problems, and successes, they see themselves in the others, trust develops, and they become more willing to open up and to be critical in their questions and responses.

Summary

In this chapter we have argued that dialogue among science teachers collaborating with one another in communities of practice can generate and share knowledge of teaching. This process is what we refer to as D-CAR. It differs from conventional action research by putting aside the need to use the rigorous methods of the social sciences to determine what works and why in the science classroom. But D-CAR is more than sitting around and talking. The dialogues among science teachers need to be structured so they lead to the desired outcomes. In Chapter 5, we describe different ways in which dialogue can be initiated and sustained, and in Chapter 9 we provide examples of how dialogue has been used by teachers as they engage in action research. But first we turn to exploring difficult, "wicked" educational problems, and how D-CAR can help mitigate them.

Note

1 In the US local education authorities are referred to as school districts.

References

Aloni, N. (2013). Empowering dialogues in humanistic education. *Educational Philosophy and Theory*, 45(10), 1067–1081. doi:10.1111/j.1469-5812.2011.00789.x.

Bereiter, C. (1994). Implications of postmodernism for science, or, science as progressive discourse. *Educational Psychologist*, 29(1), 3–12. doi:10.1207/s15326985ep2901_1.

Bevins, S., & Price, G. (2014). Collaboration between academics and teachers: A complex relationship. *Educational Action Research*, 22(2), 270–284.

Blake, J., & Gibson, A. (2021). Critical Friends Group protocols deepen conversations in collaborative action research projects. *Educational Action Research*, 29(1), 133–148. doi:10.1080/09650792.2020.1717568.

Clark, C. M. (ed.). (2001). *Talking shop: Authentic conversation and teacher learning.* New York: Teachers College Press.

Clift, R., Veal, M. L., Johnson, M., & Holland, P. (1990). Restructuring teacher education through collaborative action research. *Journal of Teacher Education*, 41(2), 52–62. doi:10.1177/002248719004100207.

Cochran-Smith, M., & Lytle, S. (1993). *Inside/Outside: Teacher research and knowledge.* New York: Teachers College Press.

Créplet, F., Dupouët, O., & Vaast, E. (2003). Episteme or practice? Differentiated Communitarian Structures in a Biology Laboratory. In M. Huysman, E. Wenger, & V. Wulf (eds.), *Communities and technologies: Proceedings of the First International Conference on Communities and Technologies; C&T 2003* (pp. 43–63). Dordrecht: Springer. doi:10.1007/978-94-017-0115-0_3.

Darling-Hammond, L. (1994). *Professional development schools: Schools for developing a profession.* New York: Teachers College Press.

Dewey, J. (1904). The relation of theory to practice in education. In C. A. McMurry (ed.), *The relation between theory and practice in the education of teachers: Third Yearbook of the National Society for the Scientific Study of Education, part 1* (pp. 9–30). Chicago, IL: The University of Chicago Press.

Dimmock, C. (2016). Conceptualising the research–practice–professional development nexus: Mobilising schools as 'research-engaged' professional learning communities. *Professional Development in Education*, 42(1), 36–53. doi:10.1080/19415257.2014.963884.

Elliott, J. (1991). *Action research for educational change*. Buckingham, UK: Open University Press.

Feldman, A. (1993). Promoting equitable collaboration between university researchers and schoolteachers. *International Journal of Qualitative Studies in Education*, 6(4), 341–357. doi:10.1080/0951839930060406.

Feldman, A. (1994, June). Long and serious conversations with teachers as research. Paper presented at Ethnography in Education, Amherst, MA.

Feldman, A. (1998). Implementing and assessing the power of conversation in the teaching of action research. *Teacher Education Quarterly*, 25(2), 27–42.

Feldman, A. (1999). The role of conversation in collaborative action research. *Educational Action Research*, 7(1), 125–144.

Feldman, A., & Alsultan, J. (2022). *Self-study of dialogic collaborative educational action research in an online environment*. SAGE Publications, Ltd. doi:10.4135/9781529600520.

Feldman, A., & Atkin, J. M. (1995). Embedding action research in professional practice. In S. Noffke & R. Stevenson (eds.), *Educational action research: becoming practically critical*. New York: Teachers College Press.

Feldman, A., Altrichter, H., Posch, P., & Somekh, B. (2018). *Teachers investigate their work: An introduction to action research across the professions* (3rd edition). New York: Routledge.

Feldman, A., Rearick, M., & Weiss, T. (2001). Teacher development and action research: findings from six years of action research in schools. In J. Rainer & E. Guyton (eds.), *Research on the effects of teacher education on teacher performance: Teacher education yearbook IX*. Dubuque, IA: Kendall Hunt Publishing Company.

Gordon, H. (1986). *Dance, dialogue, and despair: Existentialist philosophy and education for peace in Israel*. Tuscaloosa, AL: University of Alabama Press.

Hollingsworth, S. (1994). *Teacher research and urban literacy education: Lessons and conversations in a feminist key*. New York: Teachers College Press.

Horn, I. S., & Kane, B. D. (2019). What we mean when we talk about teaching: The limits of professional language and possibilities for professionalizing discourse in teachers' conversations. *Teachers College Record*, 121(6), 1–32. doi:10.1177/016146811912100604.

Jay, J. K., & Johnson, K. L. (2002). Capturing complexity: A typology of reflective practice for teacher education. *Teaching and Teacher Education*, 18(1), 73–85. doi:10.1016/S0742-051X(01)00051-8.

Knorr Cetina, K. (1999). *Epistemic cultures: How the sciences make knowledge*. Cambridge, MA: Harvard University Press.

Korthagen, F. A. J. (2007). The gap between research and practice revisited. *Educational Research and Evaluation*, 13(3), 303–310. doi:10.1080/13803610701640235.

Kristiansen, M., & Bloch-Poulsen, J. (2004). Self-referentiality as a power mechanism: Towards dialogic action research. *Action Research*, 2(4), 371–388. doi:10.1177/1476750304047981.

Laidlaw, M. (1994). The democratising potential of dialogical focus in an action enquiry. *Educational Action Research*, 2(2), 223–241. doi:10.1080/0965079940020207.

Lewin, K. (1946). Action research and minority problems. *Journal of Social Issues*, 2(4), 34–46.

Lieberman, A. (1986). Collaborative research: Working with, not working on. *Educational Leadership*, 43(5), 28–32.

Lowe, R. J., Turner, M. W., & Schaefer, M. Y. (2021). Dialogic research engagement through podcasting as a step towards action research: A collaborative auto-ethnography of teachers exploring their knowledge and practice. *Educational Action Research*, 29(3), 429–446. doi:10.1080/09650792.2021.1908905.

McDonagh, C., Roche, M., Sullivan, B., & Glenn, M. (2020). *Enhancing practice through classroom research. A teacher's guide to professional development*. New York and Abingdon, UK: Routledge.

McNiff, J. (2013). *Action research: Principles and practice* (3rd edition). New York and Abingdon, UK: Routledge.

McNiff, J. (2017). *Action research: All you need to know*. London and Thousand Oaks, CA: Sage Publications, Inc.

Mertler, C. A. (2019). *The Wiley handbook of action research in education*. New York: John Wiley & Sons.

Mills, G. E. (2018). *Action research: A guide for the teacher researcher* (6th edition). London: Pearson.

Mitchell, S. N., Reilly, R. C., & Logue, M. E. (2009). Benefits of collaborative action research for the beginning teacher. *Teaching and Teacher Education*, 25(2), 344–349. doi:10.1016/j.tate.2008.06.008.

Oxford Dictionaries (2021). Co-operation. Oxford University Press [online]. Retrieved October 23 from https://www.oed.com/view/Entry/41037?redirectedFrom=co-op eration#eid.

Pugach, M. C., & Johnson, L. J. (1990). Developing reflective practice through structured dialogue. In R. T. Clift, W. R. Houston, & M. C. Pugach (eds.), *Encouraging reflective practice in education* (pp. 186–207). New York: Teachers College Press.

Sagor, R. D., & Williams, C. (2017). *The action research guidebook: A process for pursuing equity and excellence in education*. Thousand Oaks, CA: Corwin Press.

Schön, D. (1983). *The reflective practitioner: How professionals think in practice*. New York: Basic Books.

Schön, D. (1987). *Educating the reflective practitioner*. San Francisco, CA: Jossey-Bass.

Stenhouse, L. (1975). *An introduction to curriculum research and development*. London: Heinemann.

Stenhouse, L. (1981). What counts as research? *British Journal of Educational Studies*, 29(2), 103–114.

Stoll, L., Bolam, R., McMahon, A., Wallace, M., & Thomas, S. (2006). Professional learning communities: A review of the literature. *Journal of Educational Change*, 7 (4), 221–258. doi:10.1007/s10833–10006–0001–0008.

Tikunoff, W. J., & Ward, B. A. (1983). Collaborative research on teaching. *The Elementary School Journal*, 83(4), 453–468. doi:10.1086/461326.

Tikunoff, W. J., Ward, B. A., & Griffin, G. A. (1979). *Interactive research and development on teaching. Final report*. IR&DT-79–11. San Francisco, CA: Far West Laboratory for Educational Research and Development.

Vangrieken, K., Dochy, F., Raes, E., & Kyndt, E. (2015). Teacher collaboration: A systematic review. *Educational Research Review*, 15, 17–40. doi:10.1016/j.edurev.2015.04.002.

Wells, G. (1999). *Dialogic inquiry: Towards a socio-cultural practice and theory of education.* Cambridge: Cambridge University Press. doi:10.1017/CBO9780511605895.

Wenger-Trayner, E., & Wenger-Trayner, B. (2015). Introduction to communities of practice: A brief overview of the concept and its uses. http://wenger-trayner.com/introduction-to-communities-of-practice/.

Zeichner, K. M., & Liston, D. P. (2014). *Reflective teaching: An introduction* (2nd edition). New York and London: Routledge.

4 Wicked Problems in Science Education

Introduction

In the previous chapters we provided an overall introduction to this book, a history of action research in science education, and an introduction to dialogic collaborative action research (D-CAR). We could now turn to how science teachers can engage in D-CAR, but first we want to make clear that we see this dialogic form of action research as more than a way to solve the technical problems that science teachers face daily. We see it being a way to mitigate the types of problems that are "wicked." Wicked problems are those that are so complex that they cannot be categorically defined or described, and have no clear-cut solutions (Rittel & Webber, 1973). Horst Rittel and Melvin Webber were planners – Rittel was a professor of design and Webber a professor of city planning. Their concept of wicked problems came from their realization that the problems they faced as designers and planners did not have simple, straightforward answers. To them, nearly all the definable, understandable, and consensual problems had been solved. As they wrote in 1973:

> The streets have been paved, and roads now connect all places; houses shelter virtually everyone; the dread diseases are virtually gone; clean water is piped into nearly every building; sanitary sewers carry wastes from them; schools and hospitals serve virtually every district; and so on.
>
> (p. 156)

In 2023, as we write this book, we see that we are still far from solving the problems Rittel and Webber (1973) identified as nearly or virtually solved. There are many homeless people in the US and elsewhere, water supplies are uncertain (e.g., the problem in Flint, Michigan), health care is uncertain for many citizens, and schools are underfunded. In 1973, many of the then known diseases had been eradicated or were treatable by antibiotics. Yet, as we've seen, new diseases including AIDS, COVID-19, and Ebola have appeared and continue to kill. When Rittel and Webber were writing their article, malaria had been controlled through the use of DDT to kill mosquitos. But even though there are ways to limit malaria, for example with the use of sleeping

DOI: 10.4324/9781003307174-4

nets, it continues to be a major disease in many parts of the world. Clearly, the problem of malaria is wicked.

Science teachers face educational and societal wicked problems. One that on the surface appears solvable, is that of producing a scientifically literate population. For example, for over 30 years science educators have promoted the idea that all students should understand the nature of science (Lederman & Druger, 1985). In the US this goal was incorporated into the National Science Education Standards (National Research Council, 1996), and became part of most states' curriculum standards. However, citizen responses to climate change and the COVID-19 pandemic suggest they do not understand the basic tenets of the nature of science, including its tentative nature (Lederman, 1999). We believe this is the case because enacting changes in teaching and learning in schools is a wicked problem, and most attempts to reform science teaching and learning do not recognize this. Instead, educational planners and policy makers, districts, schools, and teachers adhere to a model of change that Rittel and Webber found wholly inadequate for solving wicked problems. In 1973 this model was called Planning-Programming-Budgeting Systems (PPBS). The core of PPBS consisted of identifying objectives; specifying what needs to be done to meet those objectives; implementing the activities, making sure to identify what went into each, what was done, and what the outcomes were; evaluating the success of the activities to meet the objectives; and then making changes in objectives and solutions based on the evaluation (Ross, 1973). In education, we found it more than 70 years ago in the seminal book by Ralph Tyler, *Basic Principles of Curriculum and Instruction* (1949). In the 2000s we saw it promoted as *Backward Design* (McTighe & Thomas, 2003). Clearly this technical model of problem solving has been repackaged and resold over many years. One of the reasons for this is that it makes sense and it is easy to understand and learn. At first glance, it looks very much like how action research is introduced to novices. The reason for this is the problems we face in education, many of which are wicked problems, can only be addressed heuristically. But heuristic processes are difficult to define and package in a way that novices can learn. Instead, we describe them algorithmically, in a step-by-step fashion.

Characteristics of Wicked Problems

In their article, Rittel and Webber (1973) provided a list of ten characteristics of wicked problems. Of these, the first argued that one of the reasons for the failure of algorithmic models to solve complex problems is the difficulty in uncovering what the problem actually is: "There is no definitive formulation of a wicked problem" (p. 161). The most fundamental problem for science teachers is for their students to learn science. But what does it mean to learn science? The difficulty of determining this can be seen in the publication of science learning standards over the years. In the US, before the publication of the National Science Education Standards (National Research Council, 1996) and the AAAS Benchmarks (American Association for the Advancement of Science (AAAS), 1993), to learn science in schools meant learning the content in textbooks. Beginning around 1990, individual states also established science standards and used them for the basis of high-stakes examinations. As a result, the measure of having learned science became a score on the exam. In most of the world this is the same, with different types of matriculation examinations being used to determine science achievement.[1] This problem becomes more complex when we consider the nature of science and what counts as science. For example, should indigenous knowledge be part of school science; or as it has been promoted among religious groups, biblical creation? This suggests, as Rittel and Webber (1973) argue, "setting up and constraining the solution space and constructing the measure of performance is the wicked part of the problem" (p. 162).

Similarly, "every wicked problem is essentially unique" (Rittel & Webber, 1973, p. 164), and "every wicked problem can be considered to be a symptom of another problem" (Rittel & Webber, 1973, p. 165). Rittel and Webber argued that even when a wicked problem has many similarities to a previous problem, there is always the possibility of the new problem having a property that distinguishes it from the former. While it may be useful to consult how other problems have been solved, they cannot be used without modification for the new problem. In addition, it is extremely difficult to isolate cause and effect for wicked problems because they usually are connected to another problem. If we return to the problem of how to teach so students learn science, we can immediately see how the solution to this problem is dependent on many aspects of the educational situation, which makes the problem essentially unique for each teacher, and even possibly for each student. In addition, the problems of teaching and learning science are connected to other wicked problems such as poverty, racism, sexism, and the deprofessionalization of teaching. The complexity of wicked problems is their causes can be explained in multiple ways. For example, if we say students aren't achieving in science because they live in poverty, we can also point to those who have begun in poverty but have gone on to be very successful in the science, technology, engineering, and mathematics (STEM) disciplines. This may lead us to argue the problem is they aren't working hard enough, or they don't have role models in their communities, or so on. Each way we try to explain the cause of the problem leads to a different set of potential solutions.

Another characteristic of wicked problems according to Rittel and Webber (1973) is they have no stopping point. What they mean by this is the problem has no endpoint, primarily because it can't be constrained. Returning to the problem of students learning science, how do we decide how much science needs to be learned or to what degree of mastery? Do we expect all students to achieve at the highest levels? If not, does it matter which students we are okay with learning less or more? Rittel and Webber say we stop trying to solve a wicked problem because of reasons external to the problem, e.g., we run out of time, money, or patience. Or it may simply be because we say, "this is good enough." This leads to an additional characteristic, which is that the solutions to wicked problems are not definitive, for example, right or wrong, but rather better or worse, good enough, or satisfying (Rittel & Webber, 1973). When we get to the point where we stop, we can only say whether our attempted solution was good enough given the ill-defined nature of the problem and the resources available.

Because there is no stopping point or right or wrong solutions to wicked problems, there is also "no immediate and no ultimate test of a solution to a wicked problem" (Rittel & Webber, 1973, p. 163). Let's say we want to narrow our original problem of having our students learn science. One of the major goals of the US Next Generation Science Standards (NGSS) (NGSS Lead States, 2013) is for every student by grade 12 to be able to successfully engage in science and engineering practices (SEPs). This is the equivalent of the scientific competencies tested by the Programme for International Student Assessment (PISA) (PISA, 2022). Our problem could then be "what curriculum do we construct and teach that would lead to our reaching the NGSS goal for SEPs (or the PISA scientific competencies)?" In the US, not every student takes science through grade 12. They take biology, chemistry, physics, and/or earth science in different sequences and at different levels (basic, regular, honors, or advanced placement). From our perspective, to meet the SEPs goal for all students would require a radical transformation of the structure of secondary science in the US. Even if we do so, different students come into the classroom with different experiences, cultural capital (Bourdieu & Passeron, 1990; NeMoyer et al., 2020; Radulović, et al., 2020), and funds of knowledge (González et al., 2006). This suggests the curriculum would need to be tailored to the needs of individual students. It's beginning to look like our problem doesn't have a stopping point. We will most likely run out of time and money to reach this goal for all students. That means deciding whether what we've done is good enough, and good enough for which students in which schools. Because we can't come to a definitive answer to our problem, there is no way we can test whether we have achieved our goal or not.

Not only are there no immediate and no ultimate tests of solutions to wicked problems, Rittel and Webber (1973) argued "wicked problems do not have an enumerable (or an exhaustively describable) set of potential solutions" (p. 164). Wicked problems are not like Sudoku or crossword puzzles, which only have one solution. For example, in the US and elsewhere there have been mass shootings in schools. One possible solution is to make sure that no one has access to guns and similar weapons. Another possible solution is to make sure that there are armed, responsible adults in every school who would have the ability to stop the assailant. A third is to train students, administrators, staff, and students on what to do if there is an "active shooter" in the school. Many other solutions have also been proposed. Unfortunately, we can never know whether the solutions will always work because there may be ways around each of them.

Another characteristic of wicked problems is that once you take action to change the problem situation, the situation changes (Rittel & Webber, 1973).

In the previous example, every action to stop gun violence in schools changes the situation in unpredictable ways, which could open up new ways those heinous acts could occur. An example more specific to science education is that in the US, the move to having science standards and high-stakes examinations was part of what was referred to as systemic reform. As originally conceived, systemic reform of science education entailed improvements in the preparation of teachers and improvement of classroom teaching, resulting in improvement of student learning. It also included improvements in the opportunity to learn, which meant implementing social, economic, and structural changes in schools. As each part of the systemic process was pared down or removed because of lack of time and money, what was left was the idea of using high-stakes testing as a driver to improve science teaching and learning. The resulting change model is what is now known as the accountability movement. When systemic reform was first proposed, this movement didn't exist. Now, in trying to solve the problem of how we best teach science to all students, we need to factor in the power of the accountability system.

Rittel and Webber's (1973) final characteristic of wicked problems is written in terms of planning, which was their field. For science education, we can restate it as "the science teacher [or other science educator] has no right to be wrong." Of course we can be wrong in how we decide to teach our students, but when we are, it has negative effects on our students. Therefore, what Rittel and Webber are saying is that we need to consider the moral, ethical, and political aspects of the actions we take in response to the wicked problems we face as science teachers.

Jon Kolko provides a succinct way of thinking about wicked problems in his book *Wicked Problems: Problems Worth Solving* (Kolko, 2017). To Kolko, a wicked problem is a social or cultural problem that is nearly impossible to solve because of "incomplete or contradictory knowledge, the number of people and opinions involved, the large economic burden, and the interconnected nature of these problems with other problems" (p. 10). As an example, to paraphrase him, education is linked with poverty and wealth, poverty and wealth with nutrition, nutrition with the economy, and so on. Also somehow linked with this is socioeconomic status, home culture, first language, racism, sexism, colonialism, and so on. Any attempt to solve one issue without addressing the others will not solve the wicked problems that plague us and our world.

Wicked Problems in Science Education

In general, there are two types of wicked problems in science education. The first are ones related to science, technology, or engineering issues. The second are the wicked problems that are educational, in the sense that they pertain to the problems science teachers face in schools. In this section we will begin with a brief overview of this connection between science teaching and wicked problems, and then turn to wicked educational problems.

Teaching About Wicked Scientific Problems

There is a growing literature on how science teachers can address wicked science, technology, or engineering issues. For example, Marianne Achiam, Justin Dillon, and Melissa Glackin (2021) recently published the edited book *Addressing Wicked Problems through Science Education*. The focus of the book is on out-of-school education, such as in museums, zoos, aquaria, and botanic gardens. However, we believe science teachers can learn much from the book about how they can help their students learn about and address wicked scientific problems in their classrooms. The wicked problems addressed in the book include bacterial resistance to antibiotics; obesity and other lifestyle diseases; biodiversity loss and extinction; decreasing reliance on fossil fuels; natural gas production in a contested region; climate change; and sustainability. Not unexpectedly, the majority of the wicked problems relate to the use of fossil fuels and climate change. While there is growing evidence that a focus on these types of wicked problems can be highly motivating to students as we have seen in our work in environmental education (Alsultan et al., 2021a, 2021b), we believe the wicked educational problems science teachers face in their daily practice are more fundamental, and can be addressed through D-CAR.

Science teachers face wicked educational problems in two main ways. One relates to the nature of the topics they want to address in their classes. These topics are often labeled as controversial. The other goes beyond the classroom to the societal issues that impact science teaching. We begin with the former.

Addressing Controversial Topics

When science teachers attempt to teach about wicked science, technology, or engineering problems, they often face educational wicked problems because the wicked scientific problems are seen as controversial. Controversial issues are labeled "taboo" because many people take personal offense or groups are divided on the issues, and often these separate views are conflicting. These topics are typically avoided in everyday conversation, which makes advocating for one solution particularly difficult within the classroom (Evans et al., 1999; Hofman, 2011; Stradling, 1985; Wellington, 1986). Controversial issues tend to make students and teachers uncomfortable, as the topics deeply resonate with held values, to the extent that many people respond to information that confronts their values by rejection as a way of protecting their group identity and way of life (Monroe et al., 2019; Philpott et al., 2011). In his recent handbook chapter, Michael Reiss (2022) identified topics similar to those included as wicked problems in the edited volume by Achiam et al. (2021). These include "ecological issues (such as tackling the loss of biodiversity in an area), many health issues (such as the 'causes' of obesity), and issues to do with energy generation (such as whether wind power is better than gas-fired power stations for electricity production)" (Reiss, 2022, p. 403). Twenty years ago Gayford (2002) suggested the presence of controversy over an issue can influence teachers' instructional decisions. That is certainly the situation now as seen in the results of a recent study by the Rand Corporation that found

> 37 percent of teachers and 61 percent of principals reported being harassed because of their school's policies on COVID-19 safety measures or for teaching about race, racism, or bias during the first half of the 2021–2022 school year.
>
> (Woo et al., 2022, p. 2)

Global climate change (GCC) in the US is what Zimmerman and Robertson (2017) refer to as an "expert–public disagreement" controversy in which knowledgeable persons agree, and laypersons dispute the issue. Additionally, political controversy about the science of GCC may lead teachers to fear objections from administration, community members, and stakeholders (Maibach et al., 2008). The complexities of climate change science, and the controversy surrounding the topic within the US, is a wicked problem that has influenced how teachers instruct their students about GCC (Maibach et al., 2008). We have also faced its controversial nature in our work on climate change education, which has affected the way in which science teachers approach climate education.

Molly, Allan, and Katie worked with science teachers to address the wicked problem of GCC (Feldman et al., 2021; Nation, 2017; Nation & Feldman, 2021, 2022) using curriculum materials developed with funds from the US National Science Foundation (NSF) (https://climatechange.usf.edu/). During the time we were developing the materials along with the teachers, GCC was a highly controversial topic in the US. In fact, our project was singled out by US senator Rand Paul in his "Waste Report" and he tweeted "nearly half a million dollars to create a climate change video game. This game's intention? To spread alarmism and irrational fear among school children in a fun and interesting way." We found, as with many other studies related to the teaching of controversial topics, science teachers may hold certain beliefs worthy of instruction, but not act on their beliefs in their actual instruction of the content (Kinchin et al., 2009; Shi et al., 2014; Waters-Adams, 2006). None of the teachers we observed in that project implemented important aspects of the GCC curriculum including discussion and argumentation. They also did not support claims with the place-based nature of the curriculum. The science teachers instead attempted to remain "neutral" in their instruction of the controversial issue. Teacher neutrality when teaching controversial issues underestimates the extent to which dominant ("non expert or public") voices are amplified through this strategy while non-dominant ("expert") voices are silenced (Sanders, 1997; Sibbett, 2016). We believe it is important to help science teachers address controversial, wicked issues like GCC in their classrooms. One suggestion to make this happen is for science teacher educators to work with science teachers to address issues outside of their comfort zones (Ho & Seow, 2017; Schreiner et al., 2005). While those outside of the everyday world of science teaching can help in these ways, we believe it is important for science teachers to take the lead themselves by engaging with one another in small groups using methods such as D-CAR.

Wicked Societal and Educational Problems

Science teachers in many countries face similar societal issues that affect their students, schools, and themselves. These include the effects of poverty; discrimination due to race, ethnicity, or gender; learning differences among students; politicization of schooling; access to education; school curriculum design; environmental and natural resources policy; the deprofessionalization of teaching; and so on (we provide more information about this in Chapter 7). Problems related to diversity and equity have been identified in the science education research literature, as seen in the topics examined in the *Handbook of Research on Science Education* (Lederman & Abell, 2014). These include race and ethnicity; gender; differences between students' home language and that of their school; learning disabilities; problems related to urban and rural settings; and meeting the needs of Indigenous and ethnic minority students.

The above issues and others are interconnected in ways that make alleviating their negative effects an extremely wicked problem. Science teachers often find themselves being blamed for the effects these issues have on student learning. But it should be obvious that it is not possible for individual science teachers to cure the societal ills preventing them from providing the best educational situations for all their students. But what can be done is for small groups of teachers working together to achieve small successes in their communities. While it is unlikely what they learned can be implemented on a large scale, their new understandings of their educational situations can then be shared with other science teachers, who use it to achieve small successes in their communities. This is how we see the role of D-CAR in helping to mitigate educational wicked problems.

The role of science teachers in helping to mitigate wicked educational problems begins with their classroom practice, shared and critiqued with other teachers, and made public. This happens in D-CAR when it is employed by science teachers to construct and share knowledge about how to teach, and is then shared more broadly through workshops, presentations, blogs, websites, and articles and even books.

We end this chapter with a quotation from Rufus Jones. Jones was a Quaker, and helped to found the American Friends Service Committee in 1917. In *Faith and Practice* (Religious Society of Friends, 2022), which is the guide to Quaker religious practice in Britain, he is quoted as being disillusioned about what can come out of a 1937 World Congress. He wrote "I pin my hopes to quiet processes and small circles, in which vital and transforming events take place" (p. 24.56). We believe that small groups of science teachers engaged in the process of D-CAR can result in the vital and transforming events on which Jones pinned his hopes.

Summary

Usually when science teachers engage in action research they focus on technical problems of practice, for example how to better incorporate inquiry into their laboratory activities (Booth, 2001; Sengul & Schwartz, 2020), or how to address students' misconceptions (Stovall & Nesbit, 2003; Tugel & Porter, 2010). It is much rarer for science teachers to tackle the more complex wicked problems. In this chapter we provided an entry into the realm of scientific and educational wicked problems. Science teachers may choose to use scientific wicked problems as a way to address the complexity of issues that are STEM related and also tied to societal issues, like those in the book *Addressing Wicked Problems through Science Education* (Achiam et al., 2021). They may even be controversial in nature. D-CAR can be used by science teachers to investigate ways to incorporate these types of wicked problems into their teaching. Educational wicked problems are those that relate to the milieu in which science teaching and learning take place. These types of issues, which we have discussed in this chapter, are much more difficult for teachers to impact. We've argued in this chapter that when science teachers engage in action research in collaborative groups that use a conversational mode of inquiry, they can find ways to mitigate some aspects of these wicked problems. In doing so, science teachers need to pay attention to the moral, ethical, and political issues that affect their teaching and their students' learning.

Note

1 The TIMSS Encyclopedia provides overviews of science curricula in more than 50 countries. It is part of the TIMSS and PERLS International Study Center, which has collected and analyzed data about science programs and learning since 1995 (https://timssandpirls.bc.edu/timss-landing.html)

References

Achiam, M., Dillon, J., & Glackin, M. (eds.). (2021). *Addressing wicked problems through science education*. Dordrecht: Springer. doi:10.1007/978-3-030-74266-9.

Alsultan, J., Henderson, M., Feldman, A., Rice, M., Yang, X., Kahler, J., Ergas, S. J., & Ghebremichael, K. (2021a). Participation of high school students in authentic science and engineering experiences with a university-based water research team. *Water*, 13(13), 1745. https://www.mdpi.com/2073-4441/13/13/1745.

Alsultan, J., Rice, M., Feldman, A., Nkrumah, T., Ergas, S., & Ghebremichael, K. (2021b). Biosand filters for water purification. *The Science Teacher*, 88(4), 41–46.

American Association for the Advancement of Science (AAAS) (1993). *Benchmarks for science literacy*. New York and Oxford: Oxford University Press.

Booth, G. (2001). Is inquiry the answer? *The Science Teacher*, 68(7), 57–59.

Bourdieu, P., & Passeron, J. C. (1990). *Reproduction in education, society and culture* (vol. 4). London and Thousand Oaks, CA: Sage

Evans, R. W., Avery, P. G., & Pederson, P. V. (1999). Taboo topics: Cultural restraint on teaching social issues. *The Social Studies*, 90(5), 218–224.

Feldman, A., Nation, M., & Laux, K. (2021). The effects of extended action research-based professional development on the teaching of climate science. *Educational Action Research*, 30(4), 1–17. doi:10.1080/09650792.2021.1981417.

Gayford, C. (2002). Controversial environmental issues: A case study for the professional development of science teachers. *International Journal of Science Education*, 24(11), 1191–1200. doi:10.1080/09500690210134866.

González, N., Moll, L. C., & Amanti, C. (2006). *Funds of knowledge: Theorizing practices in households, communities, and classrooms.* New York and Abingdon, UK: Routledge

Ho, L.-C., & Seow, T. (2017). Disciplinary boundaries and climate change education: Teachers' conceptions of climate change education in the Philippines and Singapore. *International Research in Geographical and Environmental Education*, 26(3), 240–252. doi:10.1080/10382046.2017.1330038.

Hoffman, A. J. (2011). Talking past each other? Cultural framing of skeptical and convinced logics in the climate change debate. *Organization & Environment*, 24(1), 3–33. doi:10.1177/1086026611404336.

Kinchin, I. M., Hatzipanagos, S., & Turner, N. (2009). Epistemological separation of research and teaching among graduate teaching assistants. *Journal of Further and Higher Education*, 33(1), 45–55. doi:10.1080/03098770802638267.

Kolko, J. (2017). *Wicked problems: Problems worth solving.* Austin, TX: Austin Center for Design. https://www.wickedproblems.com/.

Lederman, N. G. (1999). Teachers' understanding of the nature of science and classroom practice: Factors that facilitate or impede the relationship. *Journal of Research in Science Teaching*, 36(8), 916–929doi:10.1002/(SICI)1098–2736(199910)36:8<916:AID-TEA2>3.0.CO;2-A.

Lederman, N. G., & Abell, S. K. (2014). *Handbook of research on science education* (vol. 2). New York and Abingdon, UK: Routledge.

Lederman, N., & Druger, M. (1985). Classroom factors related to changes in students' conceptions of the nature of science. *Journal of Research in Science Teaching*, 22(7), 649–662. doi:10.1002/tea.3660220705.

Maibach, E. W., Roser-Renouf, C., & Leiserowitz, A. (2008). Communication and marketing as climate change–intervention assets: a public health perspective. *American Journal of Preventive Medicine*, 35(5), 488–500. doi:10.1016/j.amepre.2008.08.016.

McTighe, J., & Thomas, R. S. (2003). Backward design for forward action. *Educational Leadership*, 60(5), 52–55.

Monroe, M. C., Plate, R. R., Oxarart, A., Bowers, A., & Chaves, W. A. (2019). Identifying effective climate change education strategies: A systematic review of the research. *Environmental Education Research*, 25(6), 791–812. doi:10.1080/13504622.2017.1360842.

Nation, M. T. (2017). *How teachers' beliefs about climate change influence their instruction, student understanding, and willingness to take action.* Dissertation, University of South Florida, Tampa, FL. https://search.proquest.com/docview/1949401046?accountid=14745.

Nation, M. T., & Feldman, A. (2021). Environmental education in the secondary science classroom: How teachers' beliefs influence their instruction of climate change. *Journal of Science Teacher Education*, 32(5), 481–499. doi:10.1080/1046560X.2020.1854968.

Nation, M. T., & Feldman, A. (2022). Climate change and political controversy in the science classroom. *Science & Education*, 31(6), 1567–1583. doi:10.1007/s11191-022-00330-6.

National Research Council (1996). *National science education standards.* Washington, DC: National Academies Press.

NeMoyer, A., Nakash, O., Fukuda, M., Rosenthal, J., Mention, N., Chambers, V. A., Delman, D., Perez, G., Jr., Green, J. G., Trickett, E., & Alegría, M. (2020). Gathering diverse perspectives to tackle "wicked problems": Racial/ethnic disproportionality in educational placement. *American Journal of Community Psychology,* 65(1–2), 44–62. doi:10.1002/ajcp.12349.

NGSS Lead States (2013). *Next Generation Science Standards: For states, by states.* Washington, DC: National Academies Press. http://www.nextgenscience.org.

Philpott, S., Clabough, J., McConkey, L., & Turner, T. N. (2011). Controversial issues: To teach or not to teach? That is the question. *The Georgia Social Studies Journal,* 1(1), 32–44.

PISA (2022). *Programme for International Student Assessment: Scientific Question Categories. Organisation for Economic Co-operation and Development (OECD).* Retrieved December 24 from https://www.oecd.org/pisa/test/scientific-question-categories.htm.

Radulović, M., Vesić, D., & Malinić, D. (2020). Cultural capital and students' achievement: The mediating role of self-efficacy. *Sociologija,* 62(2), 255–268.

Reiss, M. J. (2022). Learning to teach controversial topics. In J. A. Luft & M. G. Jones (eds.), *Handbook of research on science teacher education* (pp. 403–413). New York and Abingdon, UK: Routledge.

Religious Society of Friends (2022). *Quaker faith & practice* (5th edition). London: Religious Society of Friends (Quakers). https://qfp.quaker.org.uk/passage/24-56/.

Rittel, H. W. J., & Webber, M. M. (1973). Dilemmas in a general theory of planning. *Policy Sciences,* 4(2), 155–169. doi:10.1007/BF01405730.

Ross, R. F. (1973). You and the common sense of PPBS. *Educational Technology,* 13 (12), 57–59.

Sanders, L. M. (1997). Against deliberation. *Political Theory,* 25(3), 347–376. doi:10.1177/0090591797025003002.

Schreiner, C., Henriksen, E. K., & Kirkeby Hansen, P. J. (2005). Climate education: Empowering today's youth to meet tomorrow's challenges. *Studies in Science Education,* 41, 3–45.

Sengul, O., & Schwartz, R. (2020). Action research: Using a 5E instructional approach to improve undergraduate physics laboratory instruction. *Journal of College Science Teaching,* 49(4), 50–57. https://www.jstor.org/stable/27045878.

Shi, Q., Zhang, S., & Lin, E. (2014). Relationships of new teachers' beliefs and instructional practices: Comparisons across four countries. *Action in Teacher Education,* 36(4), 322–341. doi:10.1080/01626620.2014.948228.

Sibbett, L. A. (2016). Toward a transformative criticality for democratic citizenship education. *Democracy and Education,* 24(2), 1. https://democracyeducationjournal. org/home/vol24/iss2/1.

Smith, P. H. (2022). *From lived experience to the written word: Reconstructing practical knowledge in the early modern world.* Chicago, IL: University of Chicago Press. http://ebookcentral.proquest.com/lib/usf/detail.action?docID=7000414.

Stovall, G., & Nesbit, C. R. (2003). Let's try action research! *Science and Children,* 40 (5), 44–48.

Stradling, B. (1985). Controversial issues in the curriculum. *Bulletin of Environmental Education,* 170, 9–13.

Tugel, J., & Porter, I. (2010). Uncovering student thinking in science through CTS action research. *Science Scope,* 34(1), 30–36.

Tyler, R. W. (1949). *Basic principles of curriculum and instruction.* Chicago, IL: University of Chicago Press.

Waters-Adams, S. (2006). The relationship between understanding of the nature of science and practice: The influence of teachers' beliefs about education, teaching and learning. *International Journal of Science Education,* 28(8), 919–944. doi:10.1080/09500690500498351.

Wellington, J. J. (1986). *Controversial issues in the curriculum.* Oxford: Blackwell.

Woo, A., Wolfe, R. L., Steiner, E. D., Doan, S., Lawrence, R. A., Berdie, L., Greer, L., Gittens, A. D., & Schwartz, H. L. (2022). *Walking a fine – educators' views on politicized topics in schooling: Findings from the State of the American Teacher and State of the American Principal Surveys.* Santa Monica, CA: RAND Corporation. doi:10.7249/RRA1108-5.

Zimmerman, J., & Robertson, E. (2017). The controversy over controversial issues. *Phi Delta Kappan,* 99(4), 8–14.

5 How to Implement D-CAR

Introduction

In the preceding chapters we provided readers with background about dialogic collaborative action research (D-CAR) including what we mean by it, its connection with the literature on science teacher action research, and why it is particularly useful for addressing the wicked problems that permeate teachers' educational situations. In this chapter we provide methods you can employ to set up a D-CAR group and engage in the process. We do this with the help of a fictional D-CAR group. The first step is forming the group.

Starting a D-CAR Group

Annette teaches biology in a high school in a large school district in the southeastern US. The school is located in a dense urban area with a large percentage of students living in poverty. Many of the students are either immigrants or children of immigrants. For most, English is the language they've always spoken even if it is not the language spoken by their parents or guardians. Through inservice professional development (PD) programs provided by the district, Annette has learned about different ways to engage her students in inquiry, discussion, and argumentation (IDA). However, whenever she attempts to implement the methods she learned in the PD, things go wrong and she reverts to her fallback of lecturing to the students using PowerPoint. At one of the district-wide PD workshops, she met some other science teachers who were also interested in implementing methods to promote IDA. They decided to meet after school to talk about their experiences.

Five teachers came to the meeting, which was held at a local cafe. They began to share their experiences trying to use the methods they learned about in the PD. They realized there was a lot they could learn from one another. They decided to meet again in a few weeks, seeing if what they learned from their conversation would help them to encourage their students to engage in argumentation. At the next meeting, Charlotte told the group she thought about this group when she was taking part in the required professional learning community (PLC) at her school. She realized this group could accomplish what the PLC was supposed to do – help

DOI: 10.4324/9781003307174-5

them improve their teaching by learning together. Daniel agreed and thought if they were going to go about this in a systematic way, they could use some outside help. He remembered in one of his preservice teaching classes the professor had them form groups in which they read articles together, discussed them, and came up with ways they could use what they learned from them in their student teaching. He asked if it were okay to reach out to the professor to get some help to develop a structure for their group. The group agreed and he invited the professor to the next meeting.

The vignette above is an illustration of one way a D-CAR group could form. This is an example of what Betzabé Torres-Olave and Paulina Bravo González (2021) called a self-organized science teacher community (see Chapter 9 for more information about their groups). Often, science teacher action research groups are established by an outsider, like Daniel's professor. They can be established as part of a funded project (e.g., Baynes, 2016; Nelson, 2009; O'Donoghue & McNaught, 1991); a former teacher's dissertation study (e.g., Alsultan, 2021; Bradley, 2019; Capobianco, 2007; Feldman, 1996); or to promote a science education reform effort (e.g., Fazio & Melville, 2008; France et al., 2012; Laux, 2019; Pedretti, 1996; Subramaniam, 2010). What is similar about the groups cited above is they were established as a professional community of professionals who would offer honest, non-judgmental feedback.

Being Collaborative

The vignette illustrates how collaboration can begin to grow among the participants in a group. This is important because collaboration is a fundamental aspect of D-CAR, as we described in Chapter 3. In this vignette the group members teach in the same school district, but not in the same high school or the same science subject but they share a commitment to increase the amount of IDA that occurs in their classes. Collaboration can occur within one school, a district, or more widely across school districts. It can also occur across subjects and grade levels. An example of this is the vertical and horizontal groupings that are part of the Wipro Science Education Fellowship (SEF) program (Gunning et al., 2020). In the vertical grouping, science teachers are in mixed groups of level (elementary, middle, and high school) and district but within one science subject (biology, chemistry, physics, or earth science). The horizontal groups are composed of teachers at the same level, but from different districts. In horizontal high school groups, they teach different science subjects.

Participating in collaborative action research allows teachers with different backgrounds and experiences to form supportive partnerships and offer suggestions for improvement (Feldman, 1996; Lebak & Tinsley, 2010). That said, in our experience working with secondary science teachers, collaborative groups that go across schools and within the same science subject area are more successful than groups within schools. We believe this is due to the need for there to be enough group members with a strong commitment to sharing their experiences and then working to improve their practice through analysis and critical reflection (Feldman et al., 2018), which may not be possible if the group is limited to one school.

Methods for Creating Dialogic Conversations

In this section we provide a description of several ways that D-CAR groups can structure their conversational model. These include Enhanced Normal Practice (ENP), the Dialogos Method, Lesson Study, Journal Clubs, and Professional Learning Communities (PLCs).

Enhanced Normal Practice (ENP)

ENP is one of the ways D-CAR can be structured. It originated from Allan's dissertation study of a group of physics teachers who he convened to engage in action research (Feldman, 1996). He realized that although the teachers engaged in conventional action research methods, much, if not all, of the learning and construction of knowledge of practice came about through the teachers' conversations in the meetings that occurred every three weeks or so. Allan named this process "Enhanced Normal Practice" after one of the teachers asked, "how is this [action research] different from what I normally do?"

Allan saw when the Physics Teachers Action Research Group (PTARG) came together they engaged in a mélange of activities (see Figure 5.1) in which there was the telling, listening to, and questioning of each other's stories of practice. This supplied a context that made visible the educational situations in which the physics teachers were immersed, including details about particular

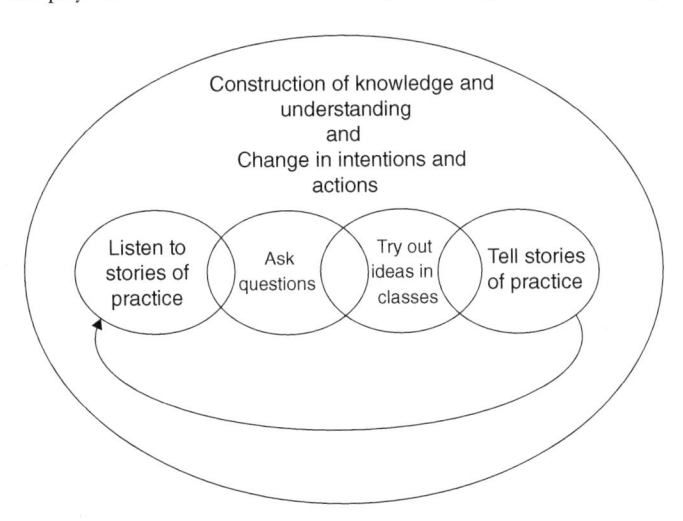

Figure 5.1 Structure of the Physics Teachers Action Research Group (PTARG).

pedagogical techniques, and ways that they and their students responded to them. As a result of these conversations, the physics teachers learned from each other about teaching methods, or came up with new ones. They then took these ideas back to their classrooms and tried them out. They paid attention to how the activity went with the students, making reflective notes as well as getting feedback from their students. The teachers then returned to the group and shared their new stories of practice based on what they did in their classes in the intervening weeks (Feldman, 1996). This led to refinement of their teaching methods and the construction of new pedagogical content knowledge.

We now return to the vignette with which we began this chapter to illustrate this process:

Charlotte came to the second meeting after having tried to engage her students in IDA using a claim-evidence-reasoning (CER) framework (McNeill & Krajcik, 2011). She told the other teachers she introduced the CER to her students and had them use it to report the results of their laboratory activity on cellular respiration. When she looked at her students' work, she was terribly disappointed. For the most part their responses were brief restatements of their observations, rather than a set of claims and explanations based on their evidence. The rest of the group listened closely to Charlotte's story of practice, and examined the examples of student work she brought with her to the meeting. They then began to ask her questions. Some asked for more information about the laboratory activity, and others about how she introduced the CER framework to the students. Other questions went more deeply. For example, Daniel wondered if the students really understood the purpose of the CER framework. Beth followed up by asking whether Charlotte had given the students any examples of what a good CER would contain. The discussion continued until the teachers decided on a plan of action. They would all try to use the CER with their students before the next meeting. They would try different ways to get their students to understand the purpose of the CER, and what good responses would look like. Then they would come to the next meeting to describe how things went and bring examples of their students' work.

The process described above and in the vignette could go on for years as teachers learn and construct knowledge together. It is possible the group could uncover a problem, dilemma, or dissonance, which they may decide to examine more closely in their practice. If so, they could choose to engage in conventional action research that we critiqued earlier in the book and provide details of in Chapter 6. However, rather than the teachers starting with the conception that action research can only be done in ways similar to those of university researchers, ENP provides the opportunity to begin, and possibly end, with the sharing and questioning of stories of practice, and the trying out of ideas, as a legitimate way to improve their practice and construct new teaching knowledge (Feldman, 1996). This is, in fact, what happened with PTARG. The group continued to meet for several years and engage in systematic inquiry without Allan. They published an article, "A Framework for

Physics Projects," about what they learned in *The Physics Teacher* (Erzberger et al., 1996).

In another example, Allan, Molly, and Katie worked with a group of high school marine science teachers engaged in D-CAR using ENP with the goal of incorporating IDA into their practice (Feldman et al., 2021). The content focus was the climate change education (CCE) materials that were developed as part of a US National Science Foundation (NSF) grant.[1] The group of teachers along with Allan, Molly, and Katie met once per month during the 2017–2018 school year. The teachers shared stories about how they used the CCE materials, returned to their classrooms to try out new ideas related to IDA, and then engaged in systematic inquiry to improve their teaching practice. Through ENP, the teachers in the study were able to incorporate IDA into their practice and gained confidence in using the CCE materials. To make this research public, one of the teachers in the study chose to publish the results of her action research on teaching about red tide in *The Science Teacher* journal (Dobson et al., 2019).

Dialogos Method of Dialogical Action Research

Another way to structure conversations is to use the Dialogos approach to action research, which was developed by Guro Helskog (2015) over a 20-year time period beginning with his exploration of the German notion of *Bildung*. *Bildung* has been defined as

> the combination of the education and knowledge necessary to thrive in one's society, and the moral and emotional maturity to be both a team player and have personal autonomy. …[it] is also the 'education' bringing this about; *Bildung* is the process as well as the result. … *Bildung* is a force of peaceful societal transformation.
>
> (Global Bildung Network, 2022)

Clearly, *Bildung* is not easily translated into English. But based on the definition above, the focus is on self-cultivation, is philosophical in nature, is an educational process, and seeks the transformation of society.

Helskog (2019) developed the Dialogos approach as a way to structure the *Bildung* process. While he refers to the dialogues in the approach as philosophical, when used in action research, they are a form of practical philosophy. Practical philosophy is concerned with aspects of everyday life including values, attitudes, and decision making. From a philosophical perspective, decision making in a field such as science teaching can be described as practical reasoning, which is the "resolving through reflection the question of what one is to do" (Wallace, 2020). It is practical because it is concerned with action, and as Wallace notes, "reflection about action itself directly moves people to act." From our discussions about action research in Chapters 2 and 3, practical reasoning could be thought of as the philosophical aspect of action research.

The Dialogos Method involves conversations with others to help people realize the practical wisdom they already have (Helskog, 2019). The focus of this method is to engage in practical reasoning through conversations to understand that thinking for yourself and thinking together are both important. The Dialogos Method as a form of *Bildung* requires a safe and trustful environment. A Dialogos dialogue may involve a facilitator who structures the conversations; however, it is important to let the conversation flow naturally, rather than planning too much ahead of time (Helskog, 2015). The method uses a structure that involves five phases: active engagement with material, choosing a focus point, philosophizing/discussing, seeking a consensus, and then individual meta-reflection. This then leads to the taking of action (see Figure 5.2).

Phase 1: In the first phase, science teachers actively engage with content. Participants are provided with an artifact such as a piece of text, a video, or a picture. It could come from outside the group, or from one of the teachers' practice. In the meeting, time is provided for the teachers to reflect individually on the artifact before discussing it with the group. This silent reflection time is important for participants to gather their own thoughts before sharing with others because inner dialogues can lead to better interpersonal dialogues (Helskog, 2019).

Phase 2: In the second phase, the science teachers choose a focus for the discussion. They write their questions and comments from phase 1 on chart paper or a whiteboard for the group to see. They then review the responses and choose one question or comment to use as a point of discussion as a

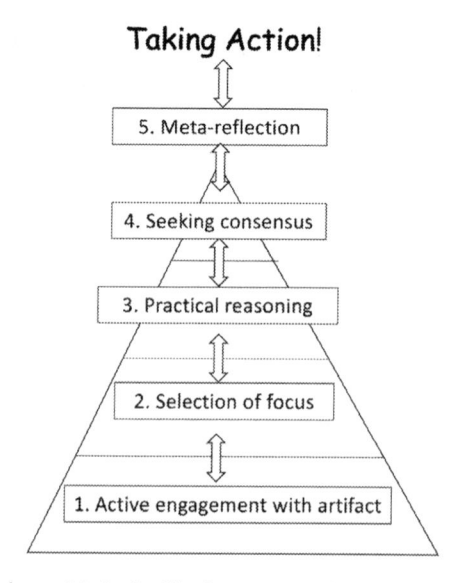

Figure 5.2 The Dialogos Method of having conversations.

group. As they make this decision, they provide reasons for choosing the question or comment.

Phase 3: The third phase of the Dialogos Method involves engaging in practical reasoning and discussing the question or comment selected in phase 2. To begin the discussion, science teachers individually come up with a way in which the question is relevant to them, possibly through an example in their practice or in their personal lives. They then share their examples and experiences with the whole group. While someone is sharing, the others try to imagine how the person feels. The facilitator writes similarities and differences between the experiences on chart paper or the board. Enough time needs to be allocated for this so there is opportunity for the expression of multiple viewpoints. This leads to conversation among the teachers about the similarities and differences among the experiences they shared.

Phase 4: In the fourth phase, the teachers seek a consensus for the discussion. Individually, teachers come up with their own one-sentence answer to the question or comment from phase 2. As a group, they try to agree on a shared answer or understanding.

Phase 5: The fifth phase is for individual meta-reflections. The science teachers engage in a silent meta-reflection on their own in which they reflect on how the experience was for them. Was it a good dialogue? How did they feel? What did they learn?

Although the Dialogos Method provides a structure for science teachers to engage in practical reasoning about their practice through reflective dialogue, it is also important for the new understandings, knowledge, and decisions to lead to changes in practice. Therefore, returning to ENP, the Dialogos approach could be thought of as a formal structure for the telling of stories of practice through the sharing of artifacts (phase 1) to identify a focus (phase 2), and discussing them through questioning (phase 3), determining next steps (phase 4), and debriefing the meeting (phase 5). Of course, after the meeting, the science teachers return to their classrooms, enact the next steps, and report on them in the next meeting (phase 1).

Lesson Study

Lesson study is another way for science teachers to come together and discuss problems of practice. The origins of lesson study can be traced back to the early 1900s in Japan (Makinae, 2010) and it was well established as a form of PD there by the 1960s (Fernandez & Yoshida, 2012). In a lesson study, a group of teachers collaborate to design a lesson. One of the teachers volunteers to implement the lesson with their students while the others observe and take notes on student learning. Rather than try to collect data on the whole class, each teacher selects a few case students to focus on. As soon as possible after the lesson, the case students are interviewed by the teachers. The interview questions should be about the students' learning, including what they enjoyed in the lesson, what they learned, what parts of the lessons helped the most, and what changes should be made if the lesson were taught again (Dudley, 2014). The student interviews are a way to include their voices in the lesson study process (Fielding, 2001; Laux, 2019). The group then collaboratively analyzes the interviews and the teachers' notes through discussion about each of the case students. They then make changes in the lesson to improve it and another one of the teachers implements the modified lesson with their students. This process can be repeated to continue to improve the lesson (see Figure 5.3).

There are many books and articles available on how to do lesson study for science teacher action researchers. We found *Lesson Study: A Handbook* by Peter Dudley (2014), *Lesson Study: A Handbook of Teacher-Led Instructional Change* by Catherine Lewis (2002), and *Collaborative Lesson Study: ReVisioning Teacher Professional Development* by Vicki Collet (2019) to be particularly useful. Science teachers may find the article "Exploring Osmosis & Diffusion in Cells" (Maguire et al., 2010) a helpful example of how a biology lesson was developed through lesson study.

While lesson study can be an effective way to improve teaching and to come to a better understanding of student learning (Fernandez & Yoshida, 2012), one of the drawbacks is the group of teachers would need to be teaching the same content at the same time. For science teachers at the secondary level, this may not be possible. Depending on the size of the school, there may be multiple science teachers who teach the same course, for example, a particular middle school grade. At the high school level, schools may have multiple biology teachers, but only one or two chemistry or physics teachers. Having an action research group that extends beyond one school can help with this issue, but at least in the US, that makes it less likely they would be teaching the same content at the same time.

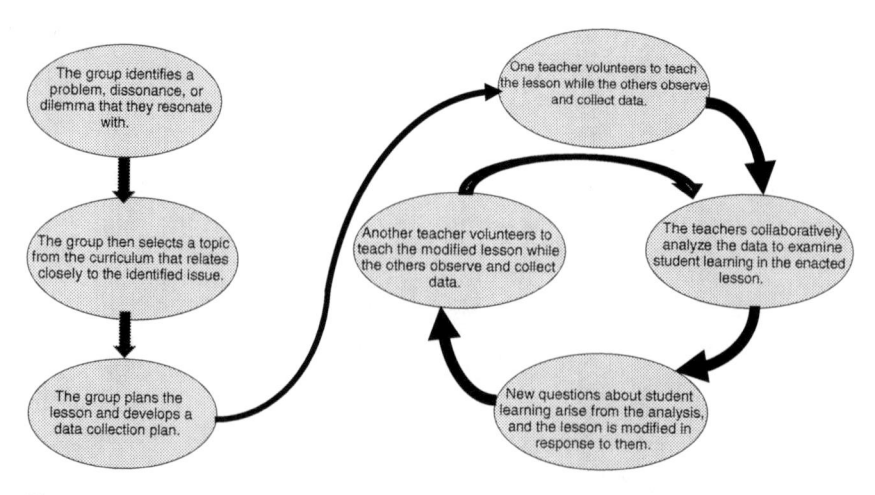

Figure 5.3 An example of a lesson study process.

Journal Clubs

A journal club is another method used to encourage dialogue that may be sustainable over time (Tallman & Feldman, 2016). In a journal club, members read journal articles related to their interests to gain a knowledge of existing research and then use this information to make improvements to their practice.

The first step of establishing a journal club is to find like-minded individuals who are interested in the same topics to join you. The second step is to establish norms or guidelines. For example, some groups may want to identify a facilitator, establish how long the meetings will last, decide how frequently they will meet, and/or determine what the focus will be. The next step is to select articles to read based on those shared interests. Finally, once the articles have been selected as a group, read and analyzed individually, the group comes together for a discussion. A presenter, who is a science teacher in the journal club, facilitates the conversation. The presenter will provide an overview of the article and use guiding discussion questions to facilitate the conversation. The questions should be developed in a way to help the group move towards solving a problem and also be specific enough to encourage conversation about the content in the article.

Professional Learning Communities (PLCs)

PLCs are another way to incorporate D-CAR into teaching practice. PLCs involve meaningful collaboration (DuFour, 2004; Lumpe, 2007) with a group of people who meet regularly to develop their knowledge of a specific topic (Wenger et al., 2002). PLCs based on the vertical articulation of content across grade levels can help teachers understand science content in other grade levels and grow as professionals (Gunning et al., 2020).

One example of how this has been implemented was when Katie held regular monthly meetings with K-12 Science, Technology, Engineering, and Math (STEM) teachers throughout the 2021–2022 school year to explore how engaging in D-CAR could support a PLC focused on discussing equity in STEM classrooms. She worked to create an environment where teachers could speak freely about how to improve equity in STEM classrooms and the implications of doing so. The PLC met virtually once a month via Zoom for about an hour. The teachers who attended these meetings were from different schools in various areas of the school district. Initially, it was challenging to engage teachers in dialogue with each other. This was addressed by incorporating nonverbal means of communicating as a way to involve them in greater discourse. Some methods of nonverbal communication included utilizing the chat feature on Zoom (https://zoom.us/), Padlet (https://padlet.com/), Microsoft Whiteboard (https://whiteboard.office.com), and Menti (https://www.mentimeter.com). Using nonverbal (and anonymous) methods of responding during meetings helped to increase participation. As the year progressed, teachers became more comfortable with verbal means of communication and began to engage in dialogue with each other. Eventually, teachers were able to have some productive conversations around equitable STEM education (see Chapter 9 for more information about Katie's project).

Unfortunately, in practice, PLCs in the US are often not really teacher communities. Instead they are teacher work groups convened by administrators to engage with school-wide or larger problems, such as increasing the numbers of students who pass high-stakes exams. In this case inquiry is focused on using the results of examinations to increase teachers' abilities and commitments to student learning by "seeing in black and white" how their students fall short of school and district examination targets (Cochran-Smith & Lytle, 2009). In addition, administrators take an instrumental view of the role of PLCs in the sense they are established to deal with particular problems. Once the problem is solved, or district priorities are changed, there is little reason for institutional support of PLCs. In Chapter 9 we provide an example in addition to Katie's of PLCs being used for a dialogic form of action research.

Other Methods for Structuring Conversations

ENP could be thought of as a method for structuring the approach a science teacher action research group takes over the course of at least several meetings. The Dialogos Method is a way of structuring individual meetings. However, there are other methods for structuring conversations that might only take a part of one meeting. We describe some of them below.

The Analytic Discourse

We begin with a method we've used quite a bit with teachers at all levels, the analytic discourse. This method was developed by Herbert Altrichter and Peter Posch (1990) in their work with teachers doing action research in Austria. It is also described in the latest edition of the book *Teachers Investigate Their Work* (Feldman et al., 2018). The purpose of the "analytic discourse" is to help action researchers gain a deeper understanding of their educational situations by engaging in a structured exchange in a small group. This method can help uncover tacit knowledge about a problem, dilemma, or dissonance teachers have identified in their practice (Feldman et al., 2018). Through the analytic discourse, a science teacher can elicit emotions surrounding the problem, and/or how to enact change based on the problem.

It is important that the analytic discourse group is not too large. We recommend between three and five participants. Each participant takes a turn providing the group with basic information about the topic to be discussed. We refer to this person as the "presenter." The group should agree on the amount of time the presenter is given to share information. In our experience, between three and five minutes works well. Part of the agreement is that all the time needs to be used. If the presenters find they have not used up all the time, they should think more about the situation and provide more details. This is especially important if the group members do not teach in the same school or district. During this first part of the analytic discourse, the other group members are not allowed to interrupt the presenter. In the second part, the rest of the group members can ask the presenter questions. Again, before the process begins, the group should come to agreement on the duration of the questioning part of the analytic discourse. This is not an open discussion; rather the group members take turns asking the presenter questions. Some basic rules about the questioning process within the analytic discourse are as follows:

- Questions should focus on helping the participant better understand the situation, the underlying theories, or to clarify the context of the problem.
- There should only be questions, no sharing stories outside of the presenter.
- Critical or judgmental questions should be avoided.
- There should be no suggestions for improvement.

After the questioning period, another group member takes a turn as the presenter. It is helpful if someone who is not the presenter be designated as a moderator to monitor adherence to the rules. The moderator should also participate in the analytic discourse process.

The Gap Activity

One of the ways we've used the analytic discourse to structure conversation is as part of the gap activity (Feldman et al., 2018). This activity arose out of Allan's teaching of a graduate course on action research. The gap is the difference between the way a science teacher would like to be as a teacher and how they see themselves now. Each teacher in the group spends a few minutes doing a free write about laying out the gap in their practice. The idea of free writing is usually attributed to Peter Elbow (1998). He developed it as a way to kickstart the writing process. To start, you begin writing and continue for a set amount of time. You do not stop for anything (it might be a good idea to set a timer). You don't worry about spelling or punctuation. You don't look back; you don't cross anything out. Elbow suggests if you can't think of what to write, write "I can't think of what to write" or just put in some squiggles. The main thing is you don't stop writing (Elbow, 1998). We usually limit the free writing to around three minutes, but it could be longer. After each person in the group writes about their gap, they then talk about it using the analytic discourse. Over the 20 years or more that Allan has used this activity with teachers at all levels, including university science faculty, only one person remarked his practice was just the way he wanted it to be and there was no gap.

Venture-Vexations

Another method of encouraging dialogue in action research groups is by using a process known as venture-vexations (Johnston & Settlage, 2008). Adam Johnston and John Settlage developed this method as part of their series of Crossroads conferences (Crossroads, undated). The main body of proposals for the conferences consists of about two pages of text divided between a venture and a vexation. In the call for proposals, the conference organizers describe vexations as specific challenges facing the proposer, including reasons why the issue is troublesome and implications of the vexation going unresolved. The venture is the course of action the proposer is considering to address the vexation. Johnson and Settlage add that the goal is to elicit conceptual, material, and emotional resources that can be used to inform next steps (Crossroads, undated).

We have used the ideas of vexations and ventures similar to ways we've used the analytic discourse but with somewhat different rules. Most importantly, we have used it in real time to engender conversation among small groups of science teachers. We begin with the venture because the teachers have already begun to examine and change their practice. We suggest group members take turns by first taking five minutes to describe what they have been doing in their classrooms (the venture) and any issues with the venture, which are the vexations. The other science teachers in the group then ask clarifying questions of the presenter. After, the group discusses the vexation while the presenter listens without interrupting. Finally, the presenter responds to comments made by the group.

Allan and Katie used this method in the past while working with science teachers in the Wipro SEF, which we described earlier in this chapter. In the second year of the program for each cohort, the teachers were required to carry out a project to help them take on leadership roles in their schools or districts. One of the ways we used to structure small group conversations was through the venture-vexation activity. The teachers reported the use of this method helped them to move their projects forward by getting past impediments stymying their progress.

The Starting Point Speech

Another activity Allan used in his teaching of the action research course is the idea of a starting point speech (Feldman et al., 2018; Feldman et al., 2021). According to Allan, this came from a conversation with Susan Noffke, whose work on action research we discuss in Chapters 2 and 8. As we've described above, the foci of conversations in D-CAR often arise from the problems, dilemmas, or dissonances in the teachers' practice. The analytic discourse, the gap, and venture-vexation activities engage the group in dialogue about those problems as a way to clarify them. A more structured way to make this happen is with the starting point speech.

In the starting point speech activity, each science teacher in the group writes a short speech, 5–10 minutes in length, and then presents the speech to the group. When we've done this either in the action research class or with groups of science teachers we've worked with, we used the analytic discourse for debriefing. The teachers then reflect on the debriefing and use it to modify their starting point for their action research. The starting point speech should include a statement of the starting point and why it is important to the science teacher's practice. It could also include any information that the teacher already has about the situation, as a result of what John Elliott (1991) calls "reconnaissance," which is either informal or formal notes about what is happening in the teacher's practice related to the starting point. Other possibilities of what to include are references to appropriate literature, thoughts about what changes the teacher might make in their practice, and any ethical concerns (Feldman et al., 2018).

The 3 C's and a Q: Compliment–Connect–Comment–Question

Jennifer Stewart-Mitchell (2020) developed the Compliment–Connect–Comment–Question discussion method as a means to engage her students in online discussions about books. Her high school students began with a blog post about the book. The other students responded with a post that included a compliment about the post; a relevant comment about the post; a connection to another text, oneself, the larger world, or to the media; and finally a question to move the conversation forward. Her article provides some examples of how her students do this. For an action research group of teachers, the three C's and a Q can be used in the same way as the analytic discourse and the venture-vexations.

Thoughts, Lingering Questions, and Epiphanies (TQE)

A method similar to the ones above was developed by another classroom teacher, Marissa Thompson (Gonzalez, 2018). As with Stewart-Mitchell, Thompson developed this method as a way to encourage her students to discuss readings. When they arrive in class, they are put into small groups in which they spend 15 minutes sharing thoughts, lingering questions, and epiphanies (TQEs). Each group then selects their top two TQEs and shares them with the whole class. Finally, there is a whole class discussion. When used with an action research group, the science teachers would choose one or more articles to read. At the next meeting the whole group would spend 15 minutes discussing the article(s) and then come to consensus on two or three TQEs.

Methods from Teaching Practice

Science teachers have developed and used various methods to engage their students in discussions. These same methods can be employed by an action research group to spur and structure conversations. In this section we review some methods we believe are appropriate for D-CAR. There are probably many more out there on the Internet. In addition, many of them can be modified to be used in online meetings through platforms such as Zoom, Teams, and Google Chat.

One of the most straightforward methods is *brainstorming*. Brainstorming involves every member of the group having the opportunity to generate ideas, comments, or questions in a set period of time; for example, five minutes. During those five minutes, there is no discussion of the ideas, praise, or criticism. In this way, all ideas are received neutrally.

In *buzz groups*, a subset of the action research group pairs off to exchange ideas, comments, and questions. There is no need to reach agreement, and they don't necessarily need to report back to the whole group.

Force-field analysis can be a next step for brainstorming or buzz groups. The aim is to uncover or identify the forces acting upon an issue from, for example, the science teachers' practice, or the students' learning or behavior. After as many forces are identified in the brainstorm or buzz groups, each is put on a sticky note and assigned a strength from 1 to 5. The sticky notes are then arranged on a large sheet of paper around the issue with forces that promote change on one side and those that inhibit it on the other. This is followed by a whole group discussion. Two other similar methods are *SWOT* analysis and *fishbone-analysis*. SWOT analysis comes from the world of business (Humphrey, 2005; Schooley, 2022). The acronym stands for strengths, weaknesses, opportunities, and threats. In this case, rather than writing the forces that impact an issue on the sticky notes, the members of the group write their thoughts about each category in SWOT. They then do the same process as with the force-field analysis. The fishbone-analysis uses a graphic organizer rather than the sticky notes (see the ConceptBoard website for details about using the fishbone-analysis: https://conceptboard.com/blog/fishbone-diagram-template-example). The first step in using it is to identify the problem, dissonance, or dilemma of practice with which the group is concerned. For example, it could be that as in the vignette above, the schools have large numbers of students who struggle with English either because it is not their first language or it is not spoken at home. That gets written in the box as seen in Figure 5.4. The next step is to brainstorm the main categories. In Figure 5.4 there are four categories: families and home culture, students, school and district policies, and teachers. The next step is to add the contributing factors. The identification of the main categories and contributing factors should be done using the brainstorming rules so everyone has the opportunity to speak their minds. After the diagram is filled in, the group discusses it to try to come to some consensus about what has been filled. The last step is to decide on next steps.

Other possible graphic organizers are *concept maps, mind maps*, and *journey maps*. Most science teachers are familiar with concept maps so we won't provide details about them here. Karen Goodnough and Robin Long (2002)

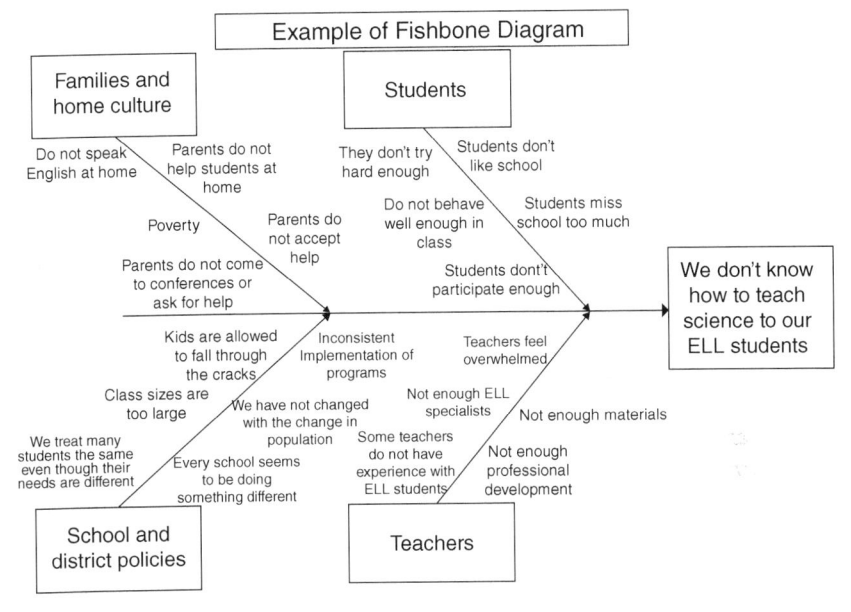

Figure 5.4 Example of the use of a fishbone diagram.
Source: Modified from https://www.doe.mass.edu/accountability/toolkit/district-data-knowledge.pdf

described how they used mind maps in a sixth grade science class for learning and assessment purposes. A *mind map* looks like a concept map, but rather than having a diagram that shows how concepts expressed in words are related to other concepts, mind maps rely on the use of images. To use it to further discussion in a D-CAR group, the first step is the same as most of the activities described above – to identify the problem, dilemma, or dissonance to focus on. A labeled, pictorial representation of that is placed in the center of the page. The next step is similar to the fishbone-analysis, which is to identify main ideas, and then add them to the diagram as a circle around the issue. Again, it helps to use some type of image to represent each of the main ideas. The group then brainstorms additional details including ideas, tasks, and questions for each main idea. Each of those is added to the diagram in a larger circle. The group could add more details in the second circle, always trying to represent them with images. Lines are then drawn from the issue in the center to each main idea and then each detail. Often the result is something like a starburst. The group then engages in a discussion of what they see in the mind map, trying to uncover new understanding from the diagram (Waida, 2022). Because this is action research, the mind map activity needs to lead to a discussion of what actions to take.

Journey maps are often individual rather than group activities. Originally developed within the world of business (see for example Agius, 2022), they are being used more frequently as both a teaching and research tool in education (Annamma, 2018; Beneke, 2021). The idea is for a science teacher, or the group together, to construct a graphical representation of the experiences that have brought them to the current situation under investigation. It is not a journey through space; rather it is one through time. That said, it may be important to include the places in which opportunities and obstacles arose, and important experiences occurred. Of course, interactions with other individuals, institutions, or organizations may need to be included to adequately map the journey. Allan started using the idea of journey maps (even though he wasn't aware they were called that) in his teaching of science methods to preservice teachers. As a way for them to explore their identities as people becoming teachers, he gave them this assignment:

> Your science teaching autobiography: Prepare a poster or other display that represents your answers to the following questions:
> - How did I get here?
> - What went into my decision to become a science teacher?
> - What was good/bad about the science classes that you were in as a student?
> - What would you do the same as a science teacher, what would you do that is different?

He also asked them to write a short description of how the display answers the questions. In the classroom setting he had the students share their displays in a poster session format. Figures 5.5 and 5.6 are examples of his students'

Figure 5.5 An example of a student's science teaching autobiography.

Figure 5.6 A second example of a student's science teaching autobiography.

displays. As with the other methods in this section, the idea is to use the journey maps as an artifact for discussions that lead to actions.

Teachers have developed a number of different ways to structure feedback so that it is constructive. One method is to give *warm and cool feedback*. We first learned of this technique from our work with the Wipro SEF project (Gunning et al., 2020). Warm feedback identifies strengths, whereas cool feedback is intended to identify issues that can promote deeper thinking about one's practice (Barber, 2007). Mark Barber reported on the use of warm and cool feedback embedded in a protocol developed by Janee Williamson, a teacher in Australia (Williamson, 2006). Her protocol, which is published in Barber's article, was designed to be used with a piece of classroom video footage selected by one of the teachers in the group. The presenter provides context, as well as highlights aspects of the video the group should pay attention to, and may also include a specific question or request for feedback. The next step is for the group to watch the video twice, taking notes of what they see as being significant. The third step is for the teachers to ask clarifying questions of the presenter, after which the group may request to view the video again. At this point each teacher provides up to three warm feedback comments to the presenter. The group does the same with the cool feedback. The presenter listens to the feedback during this step without commenting. In the next step, the presenter responds to the feedback and the rest of the group is quiet. The final steps are an open conversation about the issues raised, following by a debriefing on the process.[2]

Of course the idea of giving warm and cool feedback doesn't require the use of Williamson's protocol. The science teachers in the action research group could decide to limit themselves to warm and cool feedback during any conversation about someone's practice. A similar method is to limit feedback to *compliments and suggestions*. Compliments are similar to warm feedback. Suggestions go beyond cool feedback to provide recommendations for changes.

On-line Conversations

Over the past few years due to restrictions on gatherings because of the COVID pandemic, as well as the rapid increase in the quality of video communication apps, science teachers often find it more convenient to meet virtually rather than face-to-face. The main benefit we've seen from this is that teachers from different schools or districts don't have to travel large distances to attend the meetings in person. One of the D-CAR examples we've provided is of the COVID Community of Practice (Feldman & Alsultan, 2022) in which ten science teachers from multiple high schools met weekly in spring 2020 to develop ways to incorporate IDA into their online teaching (see Chapter 3). Because their school district is quite large, some of them would have needed to travel an hour or more to reach a central location. Given the ease in use of platforms like Zoom, it seems excessive to ask teachers to travel two or more hours roundtrip for a meeting that may be only 1 to 2 hours long. That said, we've also seen important benefits of meeting face-to-face. One technique we've used is to have the meetings rotate among the teachers' schools. That provides the opportunity for everyone to gain concrete context about each other's educational situation. It also allows for the non-verbal communication that occurs when people are in each other's presence.

We believe in many ways that this book doesn't need a special section on holding conversations online. All of the methods described above can be implemented in a virtual environment. Clearly some will take more creativity than others. However, with the ability to share and simultaneously view all types of files including text, images, video; and because of the collaboration tools built into the apps (e.g., whiteboards) and others that can be used simultaneously, D-CAR can take place virtually, as we've seen in groups in the US and Saudi Arabia. As stated earlier in the chapter, Katie used Padlet, Microsoft Whiteboard, and Menti to drive conversations with STEM teachers who met virtually. In her dissertation research, Katie also set up online journals for teachers to respond to prompts and reply to each other's responses (Laux, 2019).

Including Students/Student Voice in Research

D-CAR can engage students as well as science teachers in conversations, even though they are seldom considered equal partners in teaching and learning (Fielding, 2001; Rogers & Wright, 2007). To respect all voices in the science classroom, opportunities for dialogue among teachers and students can be provided. Science teachers can engage in action research in multiple ways to improve their practice and give students more of a participatory role in the classroom (Fielding, 2001; Lodge, 2005). To do so, student comments or responses can be sources of data, students may respond to research-related questions, or students may participate as co-researchers (Fielding, 2001). Engaging in dialogue with students about teaching practices can help teachers better understand their students' learning needs and take action (Lebak & Tinsley, 2010). Teacher–student dialogue can also help to identify and include student interest in content and pedagogical preferences. Students participating in D-CAR can have important effects on teacher beliefs and transforming teaching practices.

Katie (Laux, 2019) explored how student voice could be included in the science classroom by examining the cases of four high school teachers engaging in D-CAR. As part of her study she developed a hierarchy of participation of student voices in teachers' action research (see Figure 5.7). This was based in part on Fielding's (2001) and Lodge's (2005) models of student participation. In Katie's hierarchy, students' participation can range from being a source of information or data, to collaborating with adults and participating in research.

In the lowest level of Katie's hierarchy, science teachers would use their students as *sources of information*. This was the case of one of the teachers who

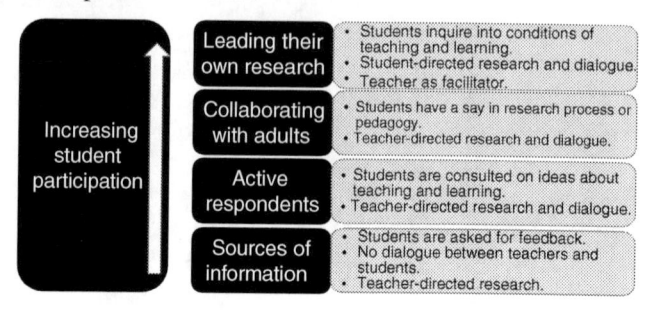

Figure 5.7 Hierarchy of student participation developed by Katie.
Source: Laux (2019).

worked with Katie. The science teacher asked for the students' ideas through surveys or questionnaires, but did not engage in dialogue with them about the data and what they meant for his teaching and their learning. Another science teacher who worked with Katie completed her action research project by engaging her students as *active respondents.* That is, they acted as active respondents where they were consulted on ideas about teaching and learning and participated in dialogue with their teacher.

In the third level of Katie's hierarchy of student participation students *collaborate with adults* in doing action research. An example of this is the Making Sense of Learning (MSL) project (Kane & Chimwayange, 2014) in which university researchers facilitated a collaboration between teachers and their students. At this level, students collaborate with teachers, and in the case of the MSL project, also with university researchers, but the action research is teacher and university researcher directed, while the students have input into the research process.

It is also possible for *students to take the lead in their own research* on learning science. The teacher acts as a facilitator, while the students direct their own inquiry into conditions of teaching and learning. We believe that this level can best be seen in what is often called youth participatory action research (YPAR) (Cammarota & Fine, 2010). YPAR is a form of participatory action research (PAR) in which young people take on the role of researcher. Alice McIntyre has argued that most PAR projects are guided by the following principles:

- the collective investigation of a problem,
- the reliance on indigenous [or local] knowledge to better understand that problem, and
- the desire to take individual and/or collective action to deal with the stated problem.

(McIntyre, 2000, p. 128)

In YPAR, the indigenous knowledge is the knowledge that youth have about the situations in which they are immersed that they are investigating. Although it is not obvious from McIntyre's principles, YPAR usually takes a critical perspective on the problems youth face. This can be seen in this definition from Julio Cammarota and Michelle Fine (2010). They state that YPAR

> provides young people with opportunities to study social problems affecting their lives and then determine actions to rectify these problems. … their research is designed to contest and transform systems and institutions to produce greater justice—distributive justice, procedural justice … in short, YPAR is a formal resistance that leads to transformation—systematic and institutional change to promote social justice.
>
> (p. 2)

Therefore, YPAR can be a method for engaging youth along with teachers in addressing the types of wicked problems we looked at in Chapter 4.

To engage with students in YPAR requires careful measures to engender trust and for stepping aside so they can be in roles that provide them with power to exercise their minds and actions. Because YPAR is not a focus of this book, we urge readers to seek assistance when engaging with students in this way. Some available resources are Mirra et al. (2015), Radina and Schwartz (2019), and the Berkeley YPAR Hub (http://yparhub.berkeley.edu).

Facilitators and Critical Friends

In this chapter we have often mentioned the role of facilitators in D-CAR. They play an important role by providing the group with resources and helping in structuring conversations. Critical friends play a similar role, but typically for an individual action researcher rather than for the whole group. Both facilitators and critical friends can be outsiders or insiders to the group.

Facilitators

Facilitators can be members of the group or outsiders. In either case they can help keep the action research group organized (Goodnough, 2003; van Oostveen, 2017) and maintain communication among members during and between meetings (Feldman et al., 2018). A facilitator can also help to set up norms prior to meetings so everyone is aware of the expectations surrounding the action research process (Fazio, 2009; Feldman et al., 2018).

Outside facilitators are more often someone who can provide resources such as access to the research literature; provide input into the answers to questions; point out problems and issues; act as a sounding board; and be an intermediary (Tripp, 1990). However, when the facilitator is an outsider, e.g., a university researcher, other issues arise due to the socially imposed hierarchy that places professors above teachers. Therefore, work needs to be done to try to make the relationship between the facilitator and science teachers as egalitarian and trustful as possible. David Tripp (1990) gives the example of finding the balance between providing too much assistance, which can possibly lessen teachers' autonomy, and withholding assistance, which could lead to making known mistakes and "reinventing the wheel." A more subtle issue can be that the facilitator, as an outsider, recognizes the impact of wicked problems that may not be of immediate interest or concern of the teachers. If the facilitator attempts to impose their view on the teachers, it could lead to a diminution of the trust between them. That said, the help of a supportive outside facilitator, who can work with teacher researcher groups with knowledge of the topics being investigated can add much to the D-CAR process (van Oostveen, 2017).

Ulrika Bergmark and her co-researchers (in press) examined the roles of mentors in action research and identified four metaphors to describe these roles: the gardener, the shepherd, the teacher, and the bridge builder. We believe these metaphors can also be used to understand the roles of facilitators. The primary purpose of the facilitator who is like a gardener is to promote good conditions for growth and learning in the action research group. This facilitator can provide advice and encouragement, and challenge the group members to reflect on their progress. The facilitator as shepherd takes on a somewhat different role from the gardener. Shepherds care for their flocks, making sure the sheep stay together and are safe. The facilitator in this role helps to guide the action research group toward an agreed upon goal without any of its members dispersing along the way. Keeping the group together provides for common experiences and learning together (Bergmark et al., in press).

Facilitators can also take on a more directive role, like being a teacher. Even when science teachers step back and make their classes student-centered, they are still the ones responsible for the students' learning. The facilitator as teacher provides background readings to inform the science teachers' action research, and provides information about different research methods and theories. It is important for this to not be a one-way street, which requires there be bridges between the facilitator and the action research group. Bridge building is especially important when the facilitator is an outsider. In the case of a facilitator who is a university researcher, bridges need to be built between the teachers, their school and community, and the university. For the bridge to serve its purpose, it should be constructed from both sides, meeting in the middle (Bergmark et al., in press).

One example of an outside facilitator working with a group of science teachers is that of Karen Goodnough (2003) who engaged in critical self-reflection on her role as a facilitator in an action research group. She facilitated weekly and, sometimes, bi-weekly meetings with teachers over the course of five months. All participants, including Goodnough, kept journals reflecting on their experience. She also openly shared thoughts and ideas with the group. She found she played different roles as a facilitator. Overall, as an organizer, she enabled the action research by managing the discourse and helping the participants develop a researcher identity. As a supporter, she encouraged participants if they became frustrated with the process and provided literature and resources as needed. As a challenger, she encouraged participants to think about issues from perspectives other than their own and allowed herself to be challenged as well. As a teacher, she shared personal experiences and educated the participants about action research and the topic of the study.

As we noted above, science teachers who are members of a D-CAR group can also be facilitators. For example, in the second year Allan worked with the PTARG teachers, he stepped back from the role of facilitator and it rotated among the members of the group. Another example is from Roland van Oostveen (2017), who worked with science and technology teachers to identify a problem to focus on for their action research and helped them write their problem statement. The teachers determined what topics they wanted to study and how they wanted to manage the meetings. The university facilitators involved in the study incorporated interventions by asking questions to help guide the action research. After the interventions, teachers began to show initiative towards their action research and were able to act as facilitators of the group. In our project with the marine science teachers (Feldman et al., 2021), we acted as facilitators to plan for meetings, help structure conversations during the meetings, and engage in our outsider research of the group's engagement in action research. We did not engage in the D-CAR ourselves, but we did take the time to have conversations amongst the research team and reflect on the meetings as we planned throughout the year.

Critical Friends

D-CAR is collaborative action research. As we've made clear above, that means the science teachers in the group are working together to help each other improve their practice and their understanding of it. One way to help one another is by taking on the role of a critical friend.

> A critical friend, as the name suggests, is a trusted person who asks provocative questions, provides data to be examined through another lens, and offers critique of a person's work as a friend. A critical friend takes the time to fully understand the context of the work presented and the outcomes that the person or group is working toward. The friend is an advocate for the success of that work.
>
> (Costa & Kallick, 1993, p. 50)

Critical friends have empathy for the other's educational situation and can relate closely to that person's concerns. As such, they are friends. However, they are also able to provide rich and honest feedback (Feldman et al., 2018). Because the relationship between the critical friend and the action researcher needs to be trustworthy, Arthur Costa and Bena Kallick (1993) suggest the action researcher needs to feel the critical friend will

- be clear about the nature of the relationship, and not use it for evaluation or judgment;
- listen well: clarifying ideas, encouraging specificity, and taking time to fully understand what is being presented;
- offer value judgments only upon request from the other;
- respond to the other's work with integrity; and
- be an advocate for the success of the work.

(Costa & Kallick, 1993, p. 50)

Clearly it takes time for this type of relationship to develop. It also requires norms to be established to set protocols for meeting and to guide conversations (Blake & Gibson, 2021). This may help to overcome some of the limitations to engaging in conversations with colleagues, such as the feeling of being at fault for facing challenges.

Because we used ENP as our approach to action research in the study with marine science teachers (Feldman et al., 2021), the role of critical friends came naturally to the study. The teachers were able to align their action research with the demands of their everyday practice and this provided them with a way to share and produce teacher knowledge. The exchanging of stories with the group gave them several critical friends to discuss ideas with and to ask for feedback. One pair of teachers were particularly well-suited for this. These two teachers worked at the same school and did much of their action research together. Prior to the study, they were already working together to plan lessons and had developed a trusting relationship that led to an effective critical friend partnership.

Summary

In this chapter, we discussed ways in which a D-CAR group could be formed and could function once the group were established. We provided a scenario of teachers working to improve their practice and discussed what "being collaborative" could look like. We provided a wide range of methods that could be used to initiate and structure dialogue and conversation within D-CAR groups. The role of student voice in D-CAR was discussed along with examples of how to include students in your action research. Finally, the role of critical friends and facilitators was described. In the next chapter we will review issues teachers may encounter while attempting to engage in action research. We will also address how to overcome some of these obstacles.

Notes

1 The materials developed by that grant can be found at https://climatechange.usf.edu/website/
2 This is very similar to the process used in the Wipro SEF project.

References

Agius, A. (2022, August 4). How to create an effective customer journey map Hub-Spot. https://blog.hubspot.com/service/customer-journey-map.

Alsultan, J. (2021). *Saudi High school science teachers' perceptions towards the integration of digital game-based learning into their teaching practice*, Dissertation, University of South Florida, Tampa, FL.

Altrichter, H., & Posch, P. (1990). *Lehrer erforschen ihren Unterricht: eine Einführung in die Methoden der Aktionsforschung.* Leipzig: Klinkhardt.

Annamma, S. A. (2018). Mapping consequential geographies in the carceral state: Education journey mapping as a qualitative method with girls of color with dis/abilities. *Qualitative Inquiry*, 24(1), 20–34. doi:10.1177/1077800417728962.

Barber, M. (2007). Imitation, interaction and dialogue using Intensive Interaction: Tea party rules. *Support for Learning*, 22(3), 124–130. doi:10.1111/j.1467-9604.2007.00459.x.

Baynes, R. (2016). Teachers' attitudes to including Indigenous knowledges in the Australian science curriculum. *Australian Journal of Indigenous Education*, 45(1), 80–90. doi:10.1017/jie.2015.29.

Beneke, M. R.,(2021). Mapping socio-spatial constructions of normalcy: Whiteness and ability in teacher candidates' educational trajectories. *Whiteness and Education*, 6(1), 92–113. doi:10.1080/23793406.2020.1803123.

Bergmark, U., Dahlbäck, A.-C., Hagström, A.-K., & Viklund, S. (in press). Leading with care: Four mentor metaphors in collaboration between teachers and researchers in action research. *Educational Action Research*.

Blake, J., & Gibson, A. (2021). Critical friends group protocols deepen conversations in collaborative action research projects. *Educational Action Research*, 29(1), 133–148. doi:10.1080/09650792.2020.1717568.

Bradley, F. B. (2019). *Exploring new teacher beliefs: Identity, home-life, and culture in the classroom*, Dissertation, University of South Florida, Tampa, FL.

Cammarota, J., & Fine, M. (2010). Youth Participatory Action Research: A pedagogy for transformational resistance. In J. Cammarota & M. Fine (eds.), *Revolutionizing education: Youth Participatory Action Research in motion* (pp. 9–20). New York and Abingdon: Routledge.

Capobianco, B. M. (2007). Science teachers' attempts at integrating feminist pedagogy through collaborative action research. *Journal of Research in Science Teaching*, 44(1), 1–32. doi:10.1002/tea.20120.

Cochran-Smith, M., & Lytle, S. (2009). *Inquiry as stance: Practitioner research in the next generation* (Vol. 24). New York: Teachers College Press.

Collet, V. S. (2019). *Collaborative lesson study: ReVisioning teacher professional development.* New York: Teachers College Press.

Costa, A. L., & Kallick, B. (1993). Through the lens of a critical friend. *Educational Leadership*, 51, 49–51.

Crossroads (undated). Science education at the crossroads. WordPress. Retrieved August 1 from http://www.sciedxroads.org/.

Dobson, A., Feldman, A., Nation, M., & Laux, K. (2019). Red tide. *The Science Teacher*, 87(1), 35–41. https://www.jstor.org/stable/26899186.

Dudley, P. (2014). *Lesson study: A handbook.* Lesson Study UK. http://lessonstudy.co.uk/wp-content/uploads/2012/03/new-handbook-revisedMay14.pdf.

DuFour, R. (2004). What is a "professional learning community"? *Educational Leadership*, 61(8), 6–11.

Lumpe, A. T. (2007). Research-based professional development: Teachers engaged in professional learning communities. *Journal of Science Teacher Education*, 18(1), 125–128. https://doi.org/10.1007/s10972-006-9018-3.

Elbow, P. (1998). *Writing without teachers* (2nd edition). New York and Oxford: Oxford University Press.

Elliott, J. (1991). *Action research for educational change.* Buckingham: Open University Press.

Erzberger, A., Fottrell, S., Hiebart, L., Merrill, T., Rappleyea, A., Weinmann, L., & Woosnam, T. (1996). A framework for physics projects. *The Physics Teacher*, 34(1), 26–28. doi:10.1119/1.2344331.

Fazio, X. (2009). Development of a community of science teachers: Participation in a collaborative action research project. *School Science and Mathematics*, 109(2), 95–107. doi:10.1111/j.1949-8594.2009.tb17942.x.

Fazio, X., & Melville, W. (2008). Science teacher development through collaborative action research. *Teacher Development*, 12(3), 193–209. doi:10.1080/13664530802259222.

Feldman, A. (1996). Enhancing the practice of physics teachers: Mechanisms for the generation and sharing of knowledge and understanding in collaborative action research. *Journal of Research in Science Teaching*, 33(5), 513–540. doi:10.1002/(SICI)1098-2736(199605)33:5<513:AID-TEA4>3.0.CO;2-U.

Feldman, A., & Alsultan, J. (2022). *Self-Study of dialogic collaborative educational action research in an online environment.* Thousand Oaks, CA: SAGE Publications. doi:10.4135/9781529600520.

Feldman, A., Altrichter, H., Posch, P., & Somekh, B. (2018). *Teachers investigate their work: An introduction to action research across the professions* (3rd edition). New York and Abingdon, UK: Routledge.

Feldman, A., Nation, M., & Laux, K. (2021). The effects of extended action research-based professional development on the teaching of climate science. *Educational Action Research*, 1–17. doi:10.1080/09650792.2021.1981417.

Fernandez, C., & Yoshida, M. (2012). *Lesson study: A Japanese approach to improving mathematics teaching and learning.* New York and Abingdon, UK: Routledge.

Fielding, M. (2001). Students as radical agents of change. *Journal of Educational Change*, 2(2), 123–141. doi:10.1023/A:1017949213447.

France, B., Mora, H. A., & Bay, J. L. (2012). Changing perspectives: Exploring a pedagogy to examine other perspectives about stem cell research. *International Journal of Science Education*, 34(5), 803–824. doi:10.1080/09500693.2011.630427.

Global *Bildung* Network (2022). *Global Bildung manifesto.* Global *Bildung* Network. Retrieved July 31 from https://www.globalbildung.net/manifesto/.

Gonzalez, J. (2018, August 4). Deeper class discussions with the TQE method. *Cult of Pedagogy.* https://www.cultofpedagogy.com/tqe-method/.

Goodnough, K. (2003). Facilitating action research in the context of science education: Reflections of a university researcher. *Educational Action Research*, 11(1), 41–64. doi:10.1080/09650790300200203.

Goodnough, K., & Long, R. (2002). Mind mapping: A graphic organizer for the pedagogical toolbox. *Science Scope*, 25(8), 20–24.

Gunning, A. M., Marrero, M. E., Hillman, P. C., & Brandon, L. T. (2020). How K-12 teachers of science experience a vertically articulated professional learning community. *Journal of Science Teacher Education*, 31(6), 705–718. doi:10.1080/1046560X.2020.1758419.

Helskog, G. H. (2015). Re-imagining 'Bildung zur Humanität': How I developed the Dialogos approach to practical philosophy through action inquiry research. *Educational Action Research*, 23(3), 416–435. doi:10.1080/09650792.2015.1013048.

Helskog, G. H. (2019). *Philosophising the Dialogos way towards wisdom in education: between critical thinking and spiritual contemplation.* New York and Abingdon, UK: Routledge.

Humphrey, A. S. (2005). SWOT analysis for management consulting. *SRI Alumni Newsletter (SRI International)* (December), 7–8.

Johnston, A., & Settlage, J. (2008). Framing the professional development of members of the science teacher education community. *Journal of Science Teacher Education*, 19(6), 513–521. doi:10.1007/s10972-008-9112-9.

Kane, R. G., & Chimwayange, C. (2014). Teacher action research and student voice: Making sense of learning in secondary school. *Action Research*, 12(1), 52–77. doi:10.1177/1476750313515282.

Laux, K. (2019). *Changing high school science teacher beliefs on student voice through action research*, Dissertation, University of South Florida, Tampa, FL.

Lebak, K., & Tinsley, R. (2010). Can inquiry and reflection be contagious? Science teachers, students, and action research. *Journal of Science Teacher Education*, 21(8), 953–970. doi:10.1007/s10972-010-9216-x.

Lewis, C. (2002). *Lesson study: A handbook of teacher-led instructional change.* Philadelphia, PA: Research for Better Schools.

Lodge, C. (2005). From hearing voices to engaging in dialogue: Problematising student participation in school improvement. *Journal of Educational Change*, 6(2), 125–146. doi:10.1007/s10833-005-1299-3.

Maguire, L., Myerowitz, L., & Sampson, V. (2010). Exploring osmosis & diffusion in cells: A guided-inquiry activity for biology classes, developed through the lesson-study process. *The Science Teacher*, 77(8), 55–60.

Makinae, N. (2010). The origin of Lesson Study in Japan. Paper presented at the Fifth East Asia Regional Conference in Mathematics Education, Tokyo, Japan.

McIntyre, A. (2000). Constructing meaning about violence, school, and community: Participatory action research with urban youth. *The Urban Review*, 32(2), 123–154. doi:10.1023/A:1005181731698.

McNeill, K. L., & Krajcik, J. S. (2011). *Supporting grade 5–8 students in constructing explanations in science: The claim, evidence, and reasoning framework for talk and writing.* Boston, MA: Pearson Allyn & Bacon.

Mirra, N., Garcia, A., & Morrell, E. (2015). *Doing youth participatory action research: Transforming inquiry with researchers, educators, and students.* New York and Abingdon, UK: Routledge. doi:10.4324/9781315748047.

Nelson, T. H. (2009). Teachers' collaborative inquiry and professional growth: Should we be optimistic? *Science Education*, 93(3), 548–580. doi:10.1002/sce.20302.

O'Donoghue, R. B., & McNaught, C. (1991). Environmental education: The development of a curriculum through 'grass-roots' reconstructive action. *International Journal of Science Education*, 13(4), 391–404. doi:10.1080/0950069910130403.

Pedretti, E. (1996). Learning about science, technology, and society (STS) through an action research project: Co-constructing an issues-based model for STS education. *School Science and Mathematics*, 96(8), 432–440.

Radina, D., & Schwartz, T. (eds.). (2019). *Radical love as resistance: Youth participatory action research for transformation.* Lakeway, TX: Sentia Publishing Company.

Rogers, R. R., & Wright, V. H. (2007). You've got mail: Using technology to communicate with parents. Unpublished paper presented at the National Educational Computing Conference, Atlanta, Georgia,

Schooley, S. (2022). SWOT Analysis: What it is and when to use it. *Business News Daily*. Retrieved August 3 from https://www.businessnewsdaily.com/4245-swot-analysis.html.

Stewart-Mitchell, J. (2020). Blogging about books. *Educational Leadership*, 77(7), 68–73.

Subramaniam, K. (2010). Understanding changes in teacher roles through collaborative action research. *Journal of Science Teacher Education*, 21(8), 937–951. doi:10.1007/s10972-010-9217-9.

Tallman, K. A., & Feldman, A. (2016). The use of journal clubs in science teacher education. *Journal of Science Teacher Education*, 27(3), 325–347. doi:10.1007/s10972-016-9462-7.

Torres-Olave, B., & Bravo González, P. (2021). Facing neoliberalism through dialogic spaces as sites of hope in science education: Experiences of two self-organised communities. *Cultural Studies of Science Education*, 16(4), 1047–1067. doi:10.1007/s11422-11021-10042-y.

Tripp, D. H. (1990). Socially critical action research. *Theory into Practice*, 29(3), 158–166.

van Oostveen, R. (2017). Purposeful action research: Reconsidering science and technology teacher professional development. *College Quarterly*, 20(2).

Waida, M. (2022, August 3). What is a mind map and how do you create one?https://www.wrike.com/blog/what-is-a-mind-map-how-to-create/.

Wallace, R. J. (2020). Practical reason. In E. N. Zalta (ed.), *The Stanford encyclopedia of philosophy*. Stanford, CA: Metaphysics Research Lab, Stanford University. https://plato.stanford.edu/archives/spr2020/entries/practical-reason/.

Wenger, E., McDermott, R. A., & Snyder, W. (2002). *Cultivating communities of practice: A guide to managing knowledge*. Boston, MA: Harvard Business Press.

Williamson, J. (2006). *Reflective tool for Intensive Interaction*. Brisbane: Red Hill Special School.

6 Engaging in Conventional Action Research

Introduction

When science teachers engage in dialogic processes such as dialogic collaborative action research (D-CAR), they share and construct knowledge that is useful, viable, and valid. This is because the new ideas and methods have been tested in real classroom situations, and have been confirmed through the sharing and questioning that takes place in the collaborative action research group. However, there may be times and situations in which science teachers may want to go beyond D-CAR to gather and analyze data to both convince themselves and others their findings are "really" valid. For example, we are currently working with a group of elementary school teachers who want to demonstrate to school district administrators that small group instruction is effective in helping students learn science. While they will be engaging in D-CAR, the administrators want to see "hard" data. Therefore, the purpose of this chapter is to provide information and methods for when science teachers choose or are required to engage in conventional action research. Because this chapter deals directly with actions science teachers could take, rather than writing it to any science teacher (our use of the third person), we switch to the second person and address you directly.

Finding a Starting Point for Research

Often the most difficult part of engaging in systematic inquiry is figuring out what it is you want to investigate. There are many ways in which to uncover some starting points we used with science teachers when we served as facilitators of action research. One of the advantages of beginning action research with D-CAR is you most likely have identified starting points that have arisen out of the discussions and conversations within the group. Therefore, many of the methods for finding starting points are the same methods we described for engendering and structuring conversations in Chapter 5.

One of the most useful tools for finding a starting point is the gap activity. When science teachers reflect on their current practice in relation to their ideal teaching practice, gaps arise that can lead to a starting point for research.

DOI: 10.4324/9781003307174-6

Another is the use of brainstorming, especially if the action research group plans to focus on the same issue. Brainstorming should result in several possible starting points. Your group can then compare and contrast them together, or even go back to their classrooms to see if the issue is really what is of importance to their situations. We also described a variety of graphic organizers in Chapter 5. Any of them could be used to help you to uncover problems of practice.

You can also use starting point speeches and elevator pitches to help to clarify or select a starting point. An elevator pitch is a short presentation – from 30 seconds to several minutes – that includes a description of the problem, dilemma, or dissonance in the educational situation and explains why it is an issue. You may also want to include any possible research methods, the hoped for outcomes, and implications for others.

Photovoice, which was developed by Carolyn Wang (1999), is a useful tool for data collection, analysis, and as a way to present action research. Basically it consists of a collection of photographs or other images with captions that illustrate some problematic aspects of schooling or a community. We describe it in detail in the data collection section below. Michael DiCicco (2014) modified the Photovoice method in a way that is useful for uncovering problems, dilemmas, and dissonances. In his method, he asks the participants to select photos or other images that are metaphors for some aspect of their practice. For example, if you are concerned about treating students differently depending on their gender, race, or ethnicity, you could select images that are metaphors for this problem. However, an important part of DiCicco's method is that the images should not include people. Once the images are selected, your group members should write a short paragraph for two to four of them explaining how each image is a metaphor for the problem. The images and paragraphs are then shared in your group with a discussion about what the images mean to the members.

Developing a Research Question

We did not mention anything about research questions in our descriptions of D-CAR. However, if you are going to engage in what amounts to conventional action research of your practice, a research question can be very useful. First, the process of developing a research question can help you to clarify the starting point. Second, the research question is a statement of the specific issue or problem that is the focus of your inquiry. It also can help to break down your project into smaller tasks making the project seem more manageable. Fourth, it can be used as the basis for the data collection plan, and therefore help you foresee possible challenges or problems. Finally, a good research question will keep you interested and focused on the topic; uncover smaller questions that need to be asked; and help to identify what resources, including background literature, you will need (Study Higher Team, 2022). In our work with science teachers incorporating authentic research in their classes, we've modified a method for developing a research question that was originally used in middle school science (Alsultan et al., 2021). Although we have not used it with teachers doing action research, one of our colleagues, Erica Dasi, has used it with undergraduate engineering students. Don't be put off by its simple nature – it works!

The structure of a research question is "how does A affect the B of C?"; where A is the independent variable, B is the dependent variable, and C is the subject of your research. For middle school and high school science students we used the following example: Suppose you are interested in what affects the quality of the water in an aquarium.

- What can we change about the quality of water? [The independent variable, A]
- What kind of data do you need to collect in order to see the effect of the independent variable on the quality of the water? [The dependent variable, B]
- The subject of the experiment is the water in the aquarium, but we could also perform an experiment on the fish or plants inside [The subject of the research, C].

Here is an example of a research question about the aquarium water quality: How does the time period between changing the aquarium water, the subject, affect the water quality? In this case the independent variable is time and the dependent variables would be the measurements to be made of the water quality. In our project at a local high school, the students measured pH, turbidity, nitrates, nitrites, and ammonia. Each of these was a dependent variable that made up the larger issue of water quality.

This same structure can be used by you to develop research questions in action research. For example, a group of science teachers may be interested in increasing students' use of argumentation in their laboratory reports; that is, their ability to argue from evidence. An independent variable could be a new teaching method. Science teachers who we work with often use a Claims, Evidence, Reasoning (CER) framework (McNeill & Krajcik, 2011) to promote argumentation. The independent variable then could be to introduce and require the use of the CER with students. The dependent variable would be a measurement of the quality of argumentation in the CER. In broad terms, the subject is the learning of argumentation skills in high school science. We also like to refer to the broad aspects of the subject as the practice situation. In Chapter 9 our summaries of science teacher action research include examples of research questions that they used.

Types of Data

Before we describe the different types of data action researchers use, we want to first provide an overview of what we mean by data. When defining a term we usually like to begin with a dictionary definition, for example, "factual information (such as measurements or statistics) used as a basis for reasoning, discussion, or calculation" (Merriam-Webster.com Dictionary, 2022). There are at least two problems with this definition for our use in action research. The first is the use of the word "factual." While there is much about teaching that can be considered factual, such as the number of students in a class, the subject being taught, or the contents of a handout, it is somewhat problematic to describe the reporting of interactions among people as factual. We address this in the next section on the ladder of inference. The second problem with the definition is the parenthetical phrase "such as measurements or statistics." Not all information is a result of measurement, and not all information can be represented through statistics. We address the latter problem in the section below on types of data.

Ladder of Inference

Because of the difficulty in determining what is a fact in social situations, we suggest you use a metaphor we use called the "ladder of inference" (Argyris, 1983; Feldman et al., 2018) that is illustrated in Figure 6.1.

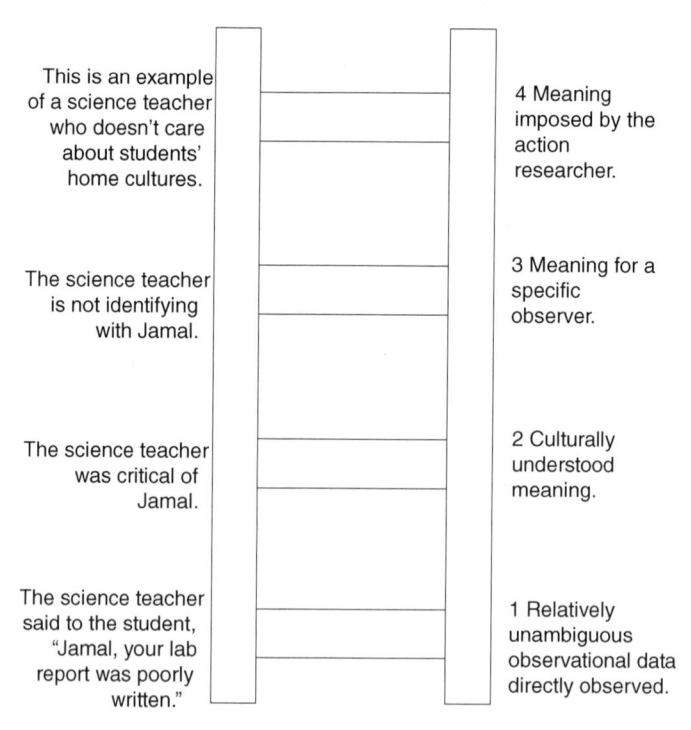

Figure 6.1 The ladder of inference.
Source: Based on Feldman et al. (2018, p. 118).

The lowest rung of the ladder is what we might call an observation. Anyone within earshot of the science teacher would most likely agree the teacher said "Jamal, your lab report was poorly written." As we go up the ladder, we ascribe more and more meaning to what was said. The meaning in rung two is one many people would agree with. To most, it may seem as if the teacher was criticizing Jamal. There would be less agreement as we head up the ladder. The meaning of the statement on the third rung is one person's opinion. Without more information, there is no way we can be sure the teacher wasn't identifying with Jamal. Finally at the top of the ladder, the action researcher is trying to get into the science teacher's head. There may be other information we can gather that supports the teacher not being caring, but caring in this sense is a state of mind that is accessible only by talking with the teacher. In general, we recommend when gathering data, it is important you try to remain as low on the ladder of inference as possible, increasing in the level of inference as you gather more data.

Before turning to the different types of data, we want to underscore the differences among observations, inferences, and facts. Most likely this is a topic you teach in your science classes. An observation can be defined as "something noticed or perceived through your senses, such as: seeing, hearing, or touching something directly" (Pruitt, 2020, p. 1). In our ladder of inference, the observation was that someone heard the science teacher say "Jamal, your lab report was poorly written." An inference is "a conclusion that is developed through evidence, reasoning, or past observations" (Pruitt, 2020, p. 1). So everything on the left side of the ladder above the observation is an inference. Another example is "I hear my dog barking." Inferences could include "there is someone outside the house" or "the dog sees a cat." Both are based on past experiences but we cannot be sure which is the correct reason for the barking unless we take a look to see what is happening. Determining whether to call something a fact or not is somewhat difficult to do. For example, the Oxford English Dictionary (2022) gives this definition of "fact":

> A thing that has really occurred or is actually the case; a thing certainly known to be a real occurrence or to represent the truth. Hence: a particular truth known by actual observation or authentic testimony, as opposed to an inference, a conjecture, or a fiction; a datum of experience, as distinguished from the conclusions that may be based on it.

In science, we tend to call something a fact when we have sufficient data to support its veracity. When dealing with human interactions, which is primarily what we do when we engage in action research, it is never clear when we have enough to warrant calling something a fact.

Data

Data are usually described as being either quantitative or qualitative, or as numbers or words. However, a better way to think of these categories is as statistical or descriptive because numerical or quantitative data can be descriptive (for example, the number of students in a class), and qualitative data can be represented in other ways than words (e.g., images). In addition, it is possible to take data that are verbal and transform them into numerical values, which can then be treated statistically. Therefore, rather than organize our discussion along the lines of quantitative or qualitative data, in the following we address data as either already existing or archival, or data that are generated.

Archival Data

Archival data are data that already exist and do not need to be generated as part of the research process. These could be results from course-based tests or assignments, or larger scale district-wide, state-wide, or national examinations. They can also be your lesson plans, student hand-outs, student work, or other documents you created, or were created by other stakeholders. For example, in the past, we've found some science teachers didn't know what the official scope of their work is. When that has been the case, we've suggested they find a copy of their individual contract or union contract, which is another type of archival data.

Generated Data

Generated data are data that do not already exist and are collected as part of the research process. For the most part there are only three ways to generate data: observations, interviews or focus groups, and surveys or questionnaires.

Observations

In some ways this is the simplest and yet most difficult type of data for science teachers to collect. After all, how do you observe yourself in action? One way to do so is to audio or video record lessons. While this may seem straightforward, usable recordings of classroom settings are very difficult to make. Our ears and eyes with the help of our brains are excellent at bracketing out extraneous information in real time. Unfortunately, when we listen or watch a recording, the background noise we didn't notice in practice can drown out what we want to listen for in the recording. One way to solve this problem is to bring the microphone close to the speaker. This can work fine, for example, in recording a teacher in a teacher-centered setting. However, then the students' voices could be difficult to hear and distinguish. When students are engaged in group activities, one recorder is not enough and the background voices can be a problem. The same problems happen with the audio of video recordings. In addition, a camera only records where it is pointed. There is technology that can help solve this problem, for example Swivl (https://www. swivl.com/), but this is an expensive solution. Another problem with recordings is they need to be listened to and/or watched, which takes time. All of this may seem like we're against the use of recordings, but they can be useful to get a sense of what is happening in your classroom or other educational situation.

The best possible way to do observations is to invite someone else into your classroom. If your action research group includes others from your school, this might be relatively easy to set up. Also, if you have a facilitator or critical friend who is a university researcher, that person may have a relatively open schedule and could come by your school. In either case, it is important to have an observation protocol. This provides guidelines for the observer about what to pay attention to. When you develop an observation protocol you should start with your research question, or other statement of the problem, dilemma, or dissonance that is your focus. From that you need to identify what needs attention. If you have a research question in the form we described above, it would be important for the observer to pay close attention to how the independent variable is being implemented, for example, the use of the CER, and the dependent variables, in this case how the students are working with the CER. The results of their use of the CER would also be a way to measure the dependent variables.

The observation protocol needs to specify what you want the observer to observe and how you want him or her to record the observations. It also needs to provide some leeway so the observer can note unexpected events. There are existing observation protocols available on the Internet. The most used one for academic research in science education is the Reformed Teaching Observation Protocol (RTOP). The RTOP was developed at Arizona State University (Sawada et al., 2002) and has been used extensively since then. There are many resources for using it, including on the website of the Science Education Resource Center at Carleton College (https://serc.carleton.edu/). Dan MacIssacs at Buffalo State College also has an informative website about the use of the RTOP: http://physicsed.buffalostate.edu/AZTEC/RTOP/RTOP_full/index.htm. You may have noticed we wrote that the RTOP has been used primarily in academic research of science teaching. It is a complex instrument and may require training in order to use it properly. However, this is not always necessary. We feel it is best used by science teacher action research researchers for ideas about what could be observed in your classroom. Horizon Research (https://www.horizon-research.com/) is another source of observation protocols and other data collect instruments. Again, you will most likely need to modify them for your purposes.

You can also carry out observations of your practice situation in real-time. The problem with this method is it is very difficult to record your observations while you are teaching. Therefore, you will most likely need to do that after the class or even after school lets out. If you use this method, we suggest you limit what it is you want to observe to one or two types of events or happenings. You may also want to focus just on particular students. You can look at other students on other days. Our memory tends to be very selective, so even if you can only jot down a few notes either during the class or right after, it would help increase the quality of the observations.

Before turning to the use of interviews, we want to provide you with information about Photovoice, which is an innovative way to obtain observational data. Photovoice was developed by Carolyn Wang (1999) in her work using participatory action research (PAR) concerning women's health issues in rural China. For our purposes, the process is simply for participants in the action research study to document their educational situation with a set of photographs and corresponding captions. In doing this, the photos and captions tell a story about the situation. Wang had three goals for her use of Photovoice, which were to enable people

> (1)to record and reflect their community's strengths and concerns; (2) to promote critical dialogue and knowledge about personal and community issues through large and small group discussions of [the] photographs; and (3) to reach policy makers.

> (Wang, 1999, p. 185)

In an action research study by science teachers on using digital photography in their practice, Allan suggested they use Photovoice to document how they were using the digital images (Feldman & Weiss, 2010). He also asked students in his science teaching methods course to document their practicum placements using Photovoice.

Hergenrather et al. (2009) in their review of the use of Photovoice as community-based PAR provide a framework (SHOWED) for discussing the photos. We've modified it for use in science teachers' action research:

1　What do you *See* here?
2　What is really *Happening* here?
3　How does this relate to *Our* practice?
4　*Why* does this problem, dilemma, or dissonance exist?
5　How can we become *Empowered through* our new understanding?
6　What can we *Do* in our practice to help resolve our problem, dilemma, or dissonance?

Of course you can use many of the methods for engendering discussion described in Chapter 5. For a detailed guide to the use of Photovoice, we suggest the book *Photovoice Research in Education and Beyond: A Practical Guide From Theory to Exhibition* (Latz, 2017).

Interviews and Focus Groups

The top rung of the ladder of inference requires getting into participants' heads. The only way to do this is to ask them questions. This could be done using surveys or questionnaires (see below), but to get nuanced answers requires the opportunity for the participant to provide open-ended responses. Most science teachers use a semi-structured interview. In this type of interview there are pre-determined questions, but you can deviate from the script. One way is to ask follow-up questions. Another is to ask for clarification, or to check to see whether you heard correctly. Usually interviews are recorded, but you can also take notes as you record. Allan has found most people like to be interviewed. It is one of the few opportunities people have where someone listens closely to what they have to say! We've found interviews with students tend to be short because they don't go into much detail in their responses. Feel free to ask for more information.

Focus groups are basically group interviews. One reason to use focus groups is that it could result in more voices being heard. However, one of the things we've found when doing focus groups with students is they sometimes are quick to agree with the first person who responds to the question. This can be avoided by directing each question to a different student.

It is important for you to have protocols for interviews and focus groups so that you are prepared with questions to ask. Because focus groups are a form of group interview, we only address interview protocols here. As with an observation protocol, you should begin with your research question, or statement of your problem, dilemma, or dissonance you are addressing. Think about who among the people in your educational situation would have the different types of information you need, for example, other teachers, administrators, students, staff members, students' families, or community members. The questions you ask each category of people will most likely be different. One way to construct questions is to brainstorm within your action research group. You can also search the Internet for existing interview protocols. Our interviews usually ask about different types of information. For example, you might want background information about a student; how much and what type of interest they have in science; or what they may have found useful or difficult about a lesson or assignment. Each of these could have multiple questions to get at the information. The last question we always ask is "is there anything else you'd like to add ... that I didn't ask about?" Interviews should not be too long. We suggest no more than half of an hour for students, and no more than one hour for adults. You should also try out the interview before you use it to gather data. If you are recording the interview, you should ask whether that is okay with the interviewee. It is important for interviewees to know the purpose of the interview and what it will entail. Therefore, begin with some introductory words. Also, don't forget to thank the interviewee at the end.

Surveys and Questionnaires

In everyday language, surveys and questionnaires are used as synonyms. However, the questionnaire is actually the equivalent of an interview protocol, whereas survey refers to the use of the questionnaire to gather data. Because questionnaires are a very common form of data collection, there is a tendency to start with them. However, we've seen it is often difficult to get people to complete questionnaires, especially if they are long. We have had many science teachers tell us about leaving questionnaires in their colleagues' mailboxes and have very few of them returned. In our experience, the best way to ensure the completion of a questionnaire is with a "captive audience." What we mean by this is if you're trying to get data from your students, ask them to fill in the questionnaire during class time and use it as an "exit slip" – something they hand in as they walk out the door. With colleagues, see if you can get some time during a faculty meeting for them to fill it out, and, again, collect them as they leave the meeting.

Related to people's reluctance to fill out questionnaires is the unlikelihood they would fill out more than one. Therefore, it is important to have a good sense of what you want to find out before developing a questionnaire, and to test it out before you administer it. In addition, as we noted above, having too many questions can greatly reduce the willingness of people to complete the survey. For one that is completely multiple choice, we recommend no more than two sides of one sheet of paper, or its electronic equivalent. A questionnaire that is all open-ended shouldn't have more than five or so questions. That said, an open-ended, online questionnaire can be an efficient replacement for an interview. While people are likely to type less than they would speak, they may also be more thoughtful in answering the questions on a web-based form. In addition, a questionnaire can be used to collect demographic information, such as number of years teaching, highest degree, and so on, rather than include those in an interview.

Of course the starting point for developing a questionnaire is with your research question, or statement of your problem, dilemma, or dissonance that you are addressing. We suggest you search the Internet for existing questionnaires related to your topic. Although you may not find one that fits your purposes exactly, existing ones can be sources of good, tested questions that can be used as is or modified. If you are going to design your own questionnaire, there are a number of preliminary decisions you need to make. These include deciding what information you need, who the target audience is, and the method of reaching the audience. You would need to then come up with the wording of the questions that will get at your needed information, and put them into an order that makes sense so they build on one another. Once you have a first draft of the questionnaire, you and a critical friend should look over it to see whether the questions actually get at what you want and that you don't have any unnecessary ones. The penultimate test is to try out the questionnaire with someone who is similar to the intended audience. For example, for questionnaires to be used with students, your own children or children of friends or relatives could be enlisted. Allan once was in a situation in which he was going to use a pre-existing questionnaire. He tested it on his nephews who were flummoxed by one of the options for a woman's job – housewife. Their mother nor any of their friends' mothers were housewives and they had never heard the term before! Finally, the more people you can get to read and take the questionnaire ahead of time will greatly enhance the likelihood that it will actually serve your purposes.

Developing a Data Collection Plan

In addressing the process of developing a data collection plan, we return to the vignette of the group of science teachers who decided to ask the question, "how does the use of the CER affect the students' ability to engage in argumentation in my science classes?" What types of data do they need to collect to answer this question? Clearly there needs to be a way to measure how well the students use argumentation skills. The source of the data could be the students' laboratory reports. However, there still needs to be a way to measure the quantity and quality of argumentation in the reports. A relatively straightforward way to do this is through the use of a rubric. In general, scoring rubrics serve the purpose of translating a qualitative perception of quality into a number. It's important to remember the numerical score from a rubric is no more accurate than teachers' ability to read students' work and assign it to different qualities of the rubric. While many science teachers make their own rubrics, there are many examples of good, and not so good, rubrics available on the Web.

In the vignette above, the teachers use the rubric as a way to measure the effects of their use of the CER. But as with the aquarium example, it's necessary to be explicit about how they use the CER and whether or not what happened in the classroom was as intended. Therefore, in this example they need a well thought out plan on how to introduce the CER to the students, as well as how to teach them to use it. In addition, the science teachers would need to collect data that confirms the plan was implemented as planned. They could do this through reflective writing, video recording of their class, or having a critical friend observe the class.

As you can see from the example above, it is important to plan out the data collection process, including what type of data to collect. One way to develop the plan is to begin again with what information is needed about the independent and dependent variables, and the practice situation. Another way to go about developing the research plan is to do the following:

First, identify the problem or question to be addressed in the action research. Then answer the following questions, making sure to answer them in order because each answer builds upon the previous one:

- What information do you need to come to a better understanding of your situation that would be the basis for good decisions about your practice situation?
- Now that you've identified the information that you need, what type(s) of data will provide you with that information?
- What types of data already exist that you can use?
- What types of data do you need to add to what already exists?
- How will you collect the data?

(Feldman et al., 2018)

Returning to the vignette, the science teachers would begin by identifying what information they need to better understand what is happening in their classrooms. Basically what this means is for them to try to describe as best as possible those aspects of their classroom situations that relate to their students' engagement in argumentation, which are the actions of the science teacher, those of the students, and the interactions between them. From the previous section we know there are four types of data that can be collected: archival data, observations, interviews, and questionnaires. The science teachers could look at archival data such as lesson plans and other materials they used to present information about how to use CERs, observations of their actions in the classroom, and/or interviews with each other. For the students, they can make observations of their students' actions in the classes, and use archival data such as their written work. The students could also be interviewed about what they know about using CERs, reasons for how they filled out the CER, and even their thoughts about argumentation in science.

At this point you may be thinking this is a lot of data, and you would be correct. While academic researchers have the luxury to collect a lot of data and analyze it over the course of months or even years, that is not usually the case for science teachers, especially if their primary goal is to improve the ways in which they use CERs to improve their current students' argumentation skills. Therefore, it is important to prioritize the types of data that would be most useful in response to the problem, dilemma, or dissonance of practice. For example, it may not be necessary to interview all the students, and possibly not any of them. Rather than interview one another, the science teachers could have a group discussion about their use of CERs, using one or more of the methods described in Chapter 5. They may find it useful to record the conversation for future reference or analysis. In any case, a data collection plan does not need to be exhaustive and certainly not exhausting.

Collecting Data – Informed Consent

Before collecting data, it is important to take into consideration that action research is almost always research on or with human subjects, i.e., other people. Therefore, it is important to pay attention to both the ethical and legal aspects related to this type of research. Often this is boiled down to the notion of informed consent. We like to parse the phrase and look first at "informed" and then "consent." It is unethical to do research with or on other people without informing them you are doing so. In a school setting this would include the students, their parents or guardians, administrators, and other teachers. Action research should not be a stealth activity. It may also be necessary to obtain consent from them. Most universities have what is called an institutional review board (IRB):

> The Institutional Review Board (IRB) is an administrative body established to protect the rights and welfare of human research subjects

recruited to participate in research activities conducted under the auspices of the institution with which it is affiliated. The IRB is charged with the responsibility of reviewing, prior to its initiation, all research (whether funded or not) involving human participants. The IRB is concerned with protecting the welfare, rights, and privacy of human subjects.

(Human Research Protection Program, 2022)

Most likely you will not need to obtain permission from a university IRB even if your facilitator or critical friend is a university researcher. That's because the university IRB is only concerned with research done by people who are affiliated with the university, so unless you are doing your action research as part of a university program it doesn't fall under its auspices. However, some school districts have their own IRB or equivalent. It's important to find out what the rules are in your district that could affect your action research. In either case, you may be required to get consent from anyone from whom you gather data. Typically written consent would be required for adults and from parents or guardians of your minor students. In addition, IRBs or their equivalents may require you to get verbal or written consent from minors. If it turns out you are not required to get written consent, there may be some situations in which you choose to do so just to make sure parents and guardians have been informed. In any case, make sure you are open about your study and inform your stakeholders of what you plan to do and why.

Analyzing Data

In the section above on data, we said they could be thought of as quantitative or qualitative, or statistical or descriptive. In this section we first provide some ways to analyze data statistically and then as descriptions.

Statistical Analysis

In general there are three broad ways to do statistical analysis. One way, which we will not discuss in our book because it is extremely rare for teachers to use, is called analysis of variance. The other two are used for testing the difference between sample-sets, and for describing samples.

Testing the Difference Between Sample-Sets

Let's say you want to compare what students in your class knew before and after you teach a lesson. One way to do this is to give them a pretest and a posttest (see Table 6.1). You could then compare how the students performed on the two tests. In order to determine whether the differences were random or due to how you taught the lesson, you may want to do a test of significance, also called hypothesis testing. In statistics the hypothesis to be tested is that your teaching made no difference. This is called the null hypothesis. The

Table 6.1 Pre- and posttest student test scores.

Student	Gender	Pretest	Posttest
A	M	75	88
B	M	65	70
C	F	78	82
D	U	82	88
E	F	95	100
F	F	50	75
G	M	45	80
H	M	62	75
I	M	58	80
J	U	82	85
K	F	85	92
L	F	62	70
M	F	74	90
N	M	72	88
O	M	68	81
P	F	40	50
Q	M	45	75
R	F	88	90
S	M	90	100
T	U	78	92
Average		70	83

Note: The gender of students who did not identify themselves as either female (F) or male (M) are classified as unspecified (U).

simplest test for doing this is called a t-test, which can be done using Microsoft Excel. Excel has instructions built in for this test, which has the formula T.TEST(array1,array2,tails,type). For the data in Table 6.1 array 1 is the pretest scores; array 2 is the posttest scores. A t-test assumes the data fit a normal distribution (also known as a bell curve). A bell curve has two tails – the lower values and the higher values. Because we don't know whether our data are skewed in one direction or the other, we will assume it has two tails. Finally there are three types of t-tests. Type 1 tests paired samples; type 2 is two different samples with equal variance; and type 3 is two different samples with unequal variance. Because we have the pre- and posttest data arranged by students, this is a paired sample and therefore type 1. When we put the values from Table 6.1 into the T.TEST formula it produced the value 4.65205×10^{-06}. This is the probability the two samples have the same mean, which is the null hypothesis. Because the average score for the pretest was 70 and for the posttest 83, this suggests there is an extremely low probability the gain in test scores was random. We can then argue that it was due to the science teacher's instruction.

You can find more help on using these types of tests on the Internet. There is even a title in the "For Dummies" series about how to do this and other types of statistical analysis using Excel: *Statistical Analysis with Excel For Dummies* (Schmuller, 2022). Another resource is the sections on statistics in Khan Academy (https://www.khanacademy.org/).

There are different types of statistical tests that can be done to compare two samples. One issue to pay attention to is that not all numerical data consist of actual numbers. For example, numerical scores from rubrics are not the same as numbers. If a student scores a five on a rubric, that is not five times better than scoring a one. Data like these are referred to as being ordinal. Ordinal data are a special case of nominal data, which consist simply as names. Examples of nominal data are gender, race, hair color, people's names, and so on. Rubric scores are nominal data that are assigned numbers so they can be ordered. Hence, they are ordinal data. Nominal and ordinal data cannot be accurately tested using a t-test. Instead, a non-parametric test needs to be used, such as the Wilcoxon Signed Rank Test. In general these are more difficult to do than a t-test, and they are not in Excel as built in functions. Again, you can find a lot of information on the Internet about doing these types of statistical tests, and there is a section on non-parametric analysis in *Statistical Analysis with Excel For Dummies*, but this may be a case where it makes sense to seek help from a statistician, such as your school's statistics teacher or a university researcher.

Descriptive Statistics

In addition to using numerical data as a way to test the effects of changes in your practice, they can also be used to describe your practice. For example, in addition to using a t-test to demonstrate that the differences between pre- and post-tests aren't random, it is possible to arrange the test scores in various ways that act to describe how the students did. You are already familiar with many ways in which this can be done, such as tables, graphs, and figures. For the pre/posttest example we've already shown ways in which the data can be represented in tables. Figures 6.2–6.4 are some ways to represent the data graphically.

Qualitative Data Analysis

We divide this section into two parts. The first deals with a relatively simple way to analyze qualitative data holistically and record the results of the analysis using memos. The other is a more formal and structured way to analyze text through the process of coding. University researchers typically use the process of coding to analyze qualitative data. According to Johnny Saldaña, a code "is most often a work of short phrase that symbolically assigns a summative, salient, essence-capturing, and/or evocative attribute for a portion of language-based or visual data" (Saldaña, 2009, p. 15). For example, in a transcript of an

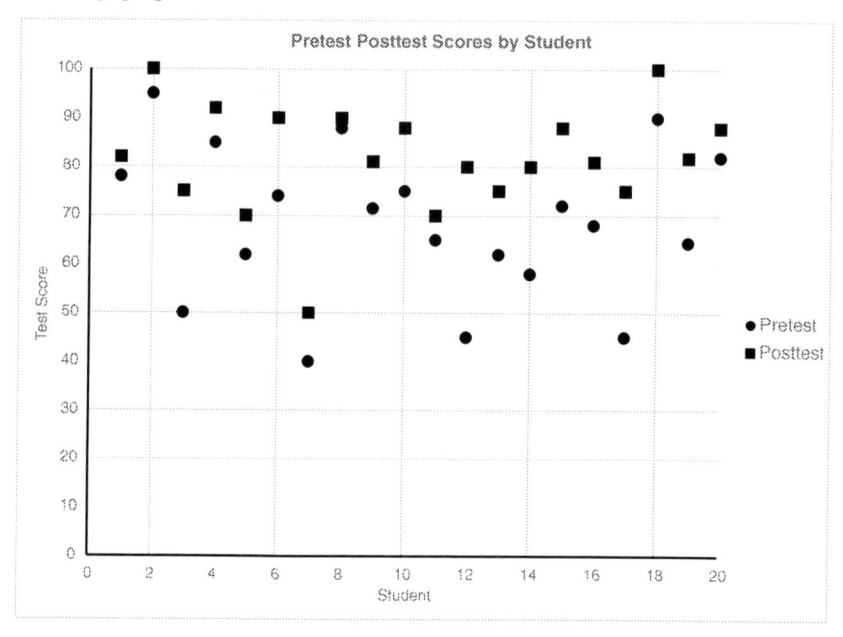

Figure 6.2 An example of how to represent student data graphically using a scatterplot.

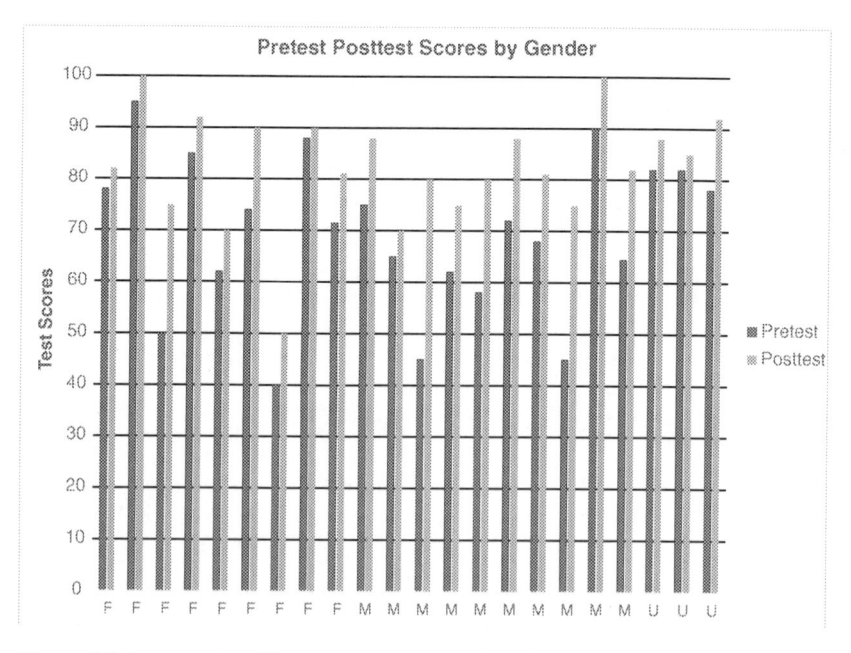

Figure 6.3 An example of how to represent student data graphically using a column chart.

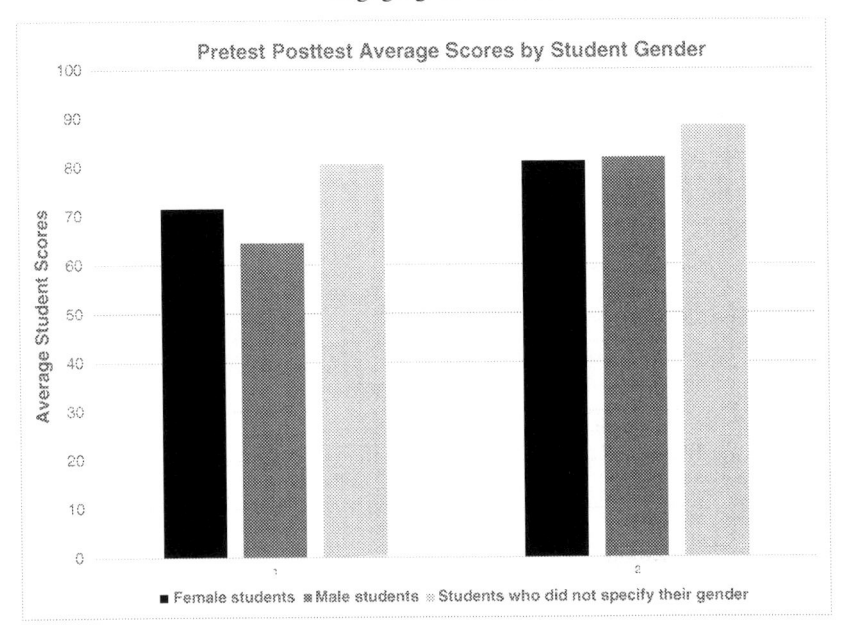

Figure 6.4. An example of how to represent average data graphically.

interview we may find something a student said to be of particular interest. In interviews we've done with high school students we have asked them if they ever had an interest in pursuing a scientific career. A student may have answered, "yes, I've always been interested in birds so I'd like to be an ornithologist." In this instance, we would assign the label "interest in science career" to this answer. That label is the code. We may also be interested in what type of career, so we may want to code the phrase as "interest in science career: ornithologist." The process of coding takes a lot of time so before we go into it in more detail, we turn to an alternative method for analyzing qualitative data that is holistic, and can be done within the time constraints felt by practicing science teachers.

Memos and Holistic Data Analysis

In data analysis, a memo is a "brief or extended narrative that documents the researcher's reflections and thinking about the data" (Miles et al., 2014, p. 95). A memo is more than a description or summary of the data. Its purpose is to record your thoughts about the meaning of the data. Memos can be written at any point in the research process, including the development of your research question, planning your data collection plan, collecting data, analyzing data, and drawing conclusions.

Saldaña (2009) provides a set of examples for how memos can be used to make sense of codes. However, he also sees them as a way to make explicit relationships between the study participants; any emergent patterns, categories, or themes; and any explanations or theories you have about what the data are saying. Each of these uses of memos can be applied to the raw data. What we are suggesting here is similar to the way in which holistic grading of written work relates to using a rubric. Coding is in some ways equivalent to using a rubric. The researcher assigns chunks of data to different codes in the same way you might read a student's written work for evidence of the degree to which the rubric's criteria are being met. Holistic grading is "the use of a scale to assign a single value mark to a whole essay and not separately to individual aspects ..." (Haswell & Elliot, 2019, p. 4). You may think of this as the old-fashioned, biased way of grading before we started using rubrics. While the use of rubrics on the surface appears to be a more consistent and less biased way to grade, holistic grading has been shown to be a reliable way to assign grades, and can even provide a better overall rating of a piece of writing. That is because rubrics only look for particular criteria and can miss more creative aspects of the writing (Haswell & Elliot, 2019).

Memos can be used to record your holistic analysis of your data. To do this you select which data you are going to analyze, read them carefully, and then record your impressions of them including any patterns you might see, ways you could categorize them and any potential ways to understand what the data are saying. Clearly this method is open to the same types of concerns people have addressed about holistic grading. The major way those concerns have been addressed is for a sample of papers to be read by two or more graders and then measuring interrater reliability – how well the graders' scoring of the papers agree. You could do this with holistic data analysis, but instead we suggest you use the power of your action research group by sharing the data and your analysis with them. This would lead to a discussion about what you saw, and how you interpreted them, and if and why the others agree with your take on them. They could also suggest alternative ways of interpreting the data.

Coding Qualitative Data

We gave a brief description of the coding process above. Before we continue, we want to make clear how time intensive this is. To code an interview requires a transcript of the interview. Typically the way that is done is to record it and then transcribe it. The recording process is relatively straightforward. Any smartphone can be used as the recording device. Then the audio file needs to be transcribed into text. There are some very good, inexpensive websites that use artificial intelligence to do the transcription. That eliminates the need to listen to the recording and type the interview. However, these automatic transcripts are not 100 percent accurate so they need to be listened to and corrected. Once you have the text, you need to go through the coding pro-cess. A 15-minute interview could take several hours to code. After you do the coding, you need to examine and group the codes into categories, and then categories into themes and then into new understandings. As you can see, this requires much more labor than the holistic analysis described above.

We believe the best way to learn how to code is to do it. That said, we provide an example of some coded text from one of our studies. In several of our projects we have tried to learn how students' engagement in authentic science activities affects their perception of science. Here is an excerpt from one of the interviews showing the codes we assigned to different portions of the text:

INTERVIEWER: In what way do you think that this project was similar to, or maybe not different from what scientists do in their daily work?

STUDENT: I think this is a very different, from, uh, your regular research at a scientific research, at a college. I don't think colleges tend to come to high schools and really work with kids a lot, Um. And I think it really builds interest, uh, for high schoolers to be involved in science in general, which is I think important this day and age. *Code: Scientists in high school*

INTERVIEWER: Actually, I was asking about how, what you did and what you've been doing, in terms of the project, how does that compare to what scientists do?

STUDENT: Um, well, compared to what I did. Um, I think that, uh, for me it's very different from, a different experience that I never experienced before. *Code: Different from school science.*

Um, I usually do things, you know, for fun and this was definitely fun, but I think, uh, there was a level of maturity, some kind of level of discipline when it came to this project specifically just because we're, we're actually doing something serious here. We're working on something that could change the lives of potentially millions of people. *Code: Real world problem.*

INTERVIEWER: So how does this compare to what you've done in your other science classes in high school?

STUDENT: Uh, compared to other science classes in high school? Um, this is a lot more inclusive and a lot more interactive than, um, a lot of many other things that I've ever done in. Usually I'm sitting in class, you know, staring at a Whiteboard, looking at problems or, you know, just listening to lectures. *Code: More hands-on than school science.*

But this is really something different. This is, you know, actual scientific research and working with the university. Um, it's very interactive. *Code: Authentic science.*

INTERVIEWER: How about how it compared to like when you have laboratory activities or experiments?

STUDENT: Well I think compared to those, uh, it's definitely more focused towards finding out something new that we haven't really tested yet. Many of the other things that I've done, I experimented, and you know, done in labs. Um, we already knew what the results were supposed to be or at least the teacher or the professor knows what the results were supposed to be.

> Those are things that have already been tested, but this is something new. It's never been tested. It's something that we can get to discover on our own. *Code: Different from school science because results weren't known ahead of time.*

In the example you can see that one of the codes is *Different from school science because results weren't known ahead of time*. For us this was a subcode of the code *Results are not known ahead of time*. By having the subcodes we were able to keep track of the different ways students felt the project was different from their usual school experience with science. As we coded the data, we found examples of students saying how it was different and in what ways that corresponded with the definition we were using for authentic science. To us, these codes could be combined into a category called "Authentic science". Another set of codes related to how the project was related to the real-world problem of shortages of potable water. We were then able to combine the category of authentic science and real-world problem in a way that led us to arrive at the theme that having a genuine, real-world problem added to the project's authenticity.

Before ending this section, we want to note there is a wealth of information about coding qualitative data on the Internet, and many how-to-do books. But as with the analysis of quantitative data, it can be very helpful to seek advice from those who have this expertise.

Triangulation

Doing action research in science education is very different from doing scientific research. In scientific research there are clear ways to establish the credibility and validity of research findings. Credibility is how believable or trustworthy the study is, while validity is how well the findings accurately reflect what is being investigated. When studying human beings in social situations it becomes much more difficult to establish what is valid or credible. In fact, there has been ongoing discussions over the years about what criteria can be used to establish the validity of qualitative research in education (Feldman, 2007; Heikkinen et al., 2007), and even whether validity should even be a goal (Eisner, 1994; Guba & Lincoln, 1981; Phillips, 1987). One way to make action research more credible or valid is through the use of triangulation.

The term triangulation was originally used to name the geometric process for locating something by observing it from two or more directions. This works because an observation defines a straight line – from the observer to the object – and two straight lines can only meet at one point. Metaphorically, triangulation in research refers to obtaining or creating multiple viewpoints based on the data, and seeking where those viewpoints converge. There are several different ways to triangulate your findings. The most common is what is called data triangulation. This means you use a variety of different data sets and compare their implications. A second type uses different interpretations of the data. These interpretations could come from the use of different theories, or simply different ways to try to understand the data. For example, the data might indicate that students from lower socioeconomic situations do not enroll in advanced science classes as much as the wealthier students. One explanation could be a difference in motivation. Another could be differences in the availability of role models in their communities. A third could be that school advisors may have biases that steer different students into different courses. Two other forms of triangulation are investigator and methodological. The former requires multiple researchers to examine the data, while the latter uses different types of methods. In recent years more researchers have been using what are called mixed-methods (Onwuegbuzie & Collins, 2007). Although there are many complicated ways to define mixed-methods research, it can be thought of as using both quantitative and qualitative research methods in the same study.

Summary

It should be clear to you at this point that engaging in conventional action research, which relies on the research methods of the social sciences, can be difficult to do while being a full-time science teacher. Not only is it a time-intensive process, but it also requires a relatively long time span to complete. As we've argued in Chapter 3, this doesn't match the rhythm and flow of teaching. It also requires expertise that is best learned through an apprenticeship-like experience in which you engage in this process along with an expert, who teaches you how to do it in manageable chunks and gives you feedback as you go along. This is what happens in courses about how to do action research, and in action research projects facilitated by university researchers. Of course, as we've noted throughout this chapter, there is an incredible amount of material about how to use these social science research methods. However, in addition to the time and expertise needed to engage in conventional action research, there are other barriers that can impede the process. We address them in the next chapter, and delve into ways in which D-CAR can help to mitigate those barriers.

References

Alsultan, J., Rice, M., Feldman, A., Nkrumah, T., Ergas, S., & Ghebremichael, K. (2021). Biosand filters for water purification. *The Science Teacher*, 88(4), 41–46.

Argyris, C. (1983). Action science and intervention. *The Journal of Applied Behavioral Science*, 19(2), 115–135. doi:10.1177/002188638301900204.

DiCicco, M. (2014). *Picturing the reader: English education pre-service teachers' beliefs about reading using Photovoice*, Dissertation, University of South Florinda, Tampa, FL.

Eisner, E. W. (1994). *The educational imagination: On the design and evaluation of school programs.* New York: Macmillan.

Feldman, A. (2007). Validity and quality in action research. *Educational Action Research*, 15(1).

Feldman, A., Altrichter, H., Posch, P., & Somekh, B. (2018). *Teachers investigate their work: An introduction to action research across the professions* (3rd edition). New York and Abingdon, UK: Routledge.

Feldman, A., & Weiss, T. (2010). Understanding change in teachers' ways of being through collaborative action research: A cultural–historical activity theory analysis. *Educational action research*, 18(1), 29–55. doi:10.1080/09650790903484517.

Guba, E. G., & Lincoln, Y. S. (1981). *Effective evaluation.* San Francisco, CA: Jossey-Bass Publishers.

Haswell, R., & Elliot, N. (2019). *Early holistic scoring of writing: A theory, a history, a reflection.* Louisville, CO: Utah State University Press.

Heikkinen, H. L. T., Huttunen, R., & Syrjälä, L. (2007). Action research as narrative: Five principles for validation. *Educational Action Research*, 15(1), 5–19. doi:10.1080/09650790601150709.

Hergenrather, K. C., Rhodes, S. D., Cowan, C. A., Bardhoshi, G., & Pula, S. (2009). Photovoice as community-based participatory research: A qualitative review. *American Journal of Health Behavior*, 33(6), 686–698. doi:10.5993/AJHB.33.6.6.

Human Research Protection Program (2022). *What is the Institutional Review Board (IRB)?*Oregon State University. Retrieved December 12 from https://research.ore gonstate.edu/irb/what-institutional-review-board-irb.

Latz, A. O. (2017). *Photovoice research in education and beyond: A practical guide from theory to exhibition.* New York and Abingdon, UK: Routledge.

McNeill, K. L., & Krajcik, J. S. (2011). *Supporting Grade 5–8 students in constructing explanations in science: The Claim, evidence, and reasoning framework for talk and writing.* Boston, MA: Pearson Allyn & Bacon.

Merriam-Webster.com Dictionary (2022). Data. Merriam-Webster, Inc. Retrieved December 8 from https://www.merriam-webster.com/dictionary/data.

Miles, M. B., Huberman, A. M., & Saldaña, J. (2014). *Qualitative data analysis* (3rd edition). Thousand Oaks, CA: Sage Publications.

Onwuegbuzie, A. J., & Collins, K. M. T. (2007). A typology of mixed methods sampling designs in social science research. *The Qualitative Report*, 12, 281–316.

Oxford English Dictionary (2022). "fact, n., int., and adv.". Oxford University Press. https://www.oed.com/view/Entry/67478?rskey=b44QlI&result=1.

Phillips, D. C. (1987). Validity in qualitative research: Why the worry about warrant will not wane. *Education and Urban Society*, 20(1), 9–24.

Pruitt, B. (2020). What do you see? Society for American Archaeology. https://www. saa.org/education-outreach/teaching-archaeology/k-12-activities-resources.

Saldaña, J. (2009). *The coding manual for qualitative researchers.* New York and Abingdon, UK: SAGE Publications.

Sawada, D., Piburn, M. D., Judson, E., Turley, J., Falconer, K., Benford, R., & Bloom, I. (2002). Measuring reform practices in science and mathematics classrooms: The reformed teaching observation protocol. *School Science and Mathematics*, 102(6), 245–253.

Schmuller, J. (2022). *Statistical analysis with Excel for dummies* (5th edition). Hoboken, NJ: John Wiley & Sons.

Study Higher Team (2022). Research question: the importance of your research question. University of Oxford. Retrieved December 6 from https://www.studyhigher. ac.uk/our-partners/university-of-oxford/bqlq-1-2-importance-research-question/#: ~:text=The%20research%20question%2C%20if%20correctly,time%2C%20energy%2C %20and%20effort.

Wang, C. C. (1999). Photovoice: A participatory action research strategy applied to women's health. *Journal of Women's Health*, 8(2), 185–192.

7 Barriers to Implementing Action Research

Introduction

In the previous two chapters we described ways in which science teachers can engage in dialogic collaborative action research (D-CAR) and conventional action research. As we noted in Chapter 6, conventional action research requires significant time commitments from science teachers as well as learning the methods of the social sciences. In addition, there are other barriers that limit using those methods. Some of these barriers relate to how science teaching is structured in the K-12 school environment in the US and elsewhere. These include time constraints related to the need to follow a set curriculum; the difficulty teachers feel in making changes in their regular modes of teaching, often referred to as resistance; and their beliefs their voices will not be heard (Mansour, 2009). Other barriers we examine in this chapter address school district and school policies that could impede doing conventional action research. While districts may say they are interested in the idea of science teachers engaging in action research, they often do not provide teachers with the needed resources to do so. In some situations where resources are available, such as time set aside for professional learning communities (PLCs), those resources are used for other priorities. Science teachers and school-based administrators may also be subject to policies created by district-level administrators and may not feel they have the freedom to focus on supporting conventional action research at their school site. Finally, lack of support from other teachers and administrators may serve as impediments to engaging in action research.

In the remainder of this chapter we describe some of the obstacles science teachers face when they attempt to engage in conventional action research. These include the deprofessionalization of teaching; constraints on science teachers' time; difficulties in changing one's practice; district and school policies; and lack of support from other faculty and/or administrators. In each section we provide ways in which the use of D-CAR can help to mitigate these obstacles.

Deprofessionalization of Teaching

Much of what we just identified as barriers are outcomes of the deprofessionalization of teaching in the US and elsewhere. Because of the educational

DOI: 10.4324/9781003307174-7

policies of countries, regions, states, and districts, science teachers are experiencing deprofessionalization in their careers, which reduces their autonomy to make decisions about what is best for their students (Carter Andrews et al., 2016; Milner, 2013). This change in the nature of the profession is reducing or eliminating many of the extrinsic and intrinsic reasons that keep teachers in the classroom (Hodges et al., 2013; Lortie, 1975). We and others are concerned the deprofessionalization of teaching will lead more independent thinking teachers to leave the profession (Hodges et al., 2013). They are often the type of teachers who would seek out opportunities to engage in dialogue to improve their practice to better support their students.

However, before discussing the deprofessionalization of teaching further, we want to delve a bit deeper into what it means to be a professional. We found the following in a chapter on teachers as professionals (Bascia, 2009):

> Professionalized occupations possess status, respect and authority and are taken seriously by government and by the public at large. A professional body or association exists, and membership is a requirement for employment. They have considerable control over the conditions of their work and latitude to decide on the best courses of action in their practice. They evaluate and disseminate exclusive occupational knowledge, and training and entry requirements are controlled by the group itself rather than by another body such as government. They, rather than government, enforce a code of occupational ethics and conduct.
>
> (p. 482)

Teaching has few of these characteristics, and as a result has been labeled a "semi-profession." Semi-professions are those in which "their training is shorter, their status is less legitimated, their right to privileged communication is less established, there is less of a specialized body of knowledge, and they have less autonomy from supervision of societal control than 'the' professions" (Etzioni, 1969, p. v). Amatai Etzioni included teaching, nursing, and social work in his list of semi-professions, noting all have very large percentages of female workers. In the years since he published this book, teaching if anything has become regarded as less of a profession as a result of government policies (Milner, 2013; Wronowski & Urick, 2021).

A major aspect of deprofessionalization of teaching is the growing trend for science teachers to be given set curricula to follow or pacing guides that determine how much time should be spent on each concept. Instructional priorities determined by state or district administrators are often focused on a scripted science curriculum, mandatory testing, and teaching to required science standards evaluated on the tests. Teachers are required to teach according to these priorities, and are then evaluated according to how well their students do on these exams (Carter Andrews et al., 2016). The purpose of preset science curricula tied to standards is to ensure all students are learning the same material. However, it also contributes to the deprofessionalization of teaching

(Hodges & Tipton, 2013; Milner, 2013). This sends the message that teaching is technical work anyone can do if they follow the script or the preset curriculum (Milner, 2013).

Districts often attempt to introduce educational reform initiatives from the top-down even though there is extensive evidence these types of change models are ineffective (Supovitz & Turner, 2000). One reason for this ineffectiveness is that district initiatives tend to be too broad to encompass the complexities of classroom teaching and do not accurately meet the reality of science teaching and learning. Therefore, school-based administrators may not feel they have the freedom to implement professional development (PD) to support conventional action research at their school site even if they feel it would be best for their teachers (Whitworth & Chiu, 2015). This may be due to district policies that prevent schools from implementing measures they feel are best for their site.

In addition, some school-based administrators do not acknowledge science teachers' pedagogical expertise even when presented with evidence, which in turn causes teachers to feel administrators are devaluing their professional knowledge (Hodges & Tipton, 2013). Faced with a standards-based curriculum focused on examination scores, it can be difficult for science teachers to stand up to administrators who do not respect their pedagogical and science content knowledge (Manley, 2008), and their ability to construct new knowledge of teaching and learning science even if doing this can lead to better learning opportunities for students.

When science teaching is deprofessionalized, there is no purpose or place for conventional action research. Conventional action research is modeled on the methods used in the construction of knowledge in the social sciences. When science teaching is operationalized as the implementation of curricula developed by outside experts to meet standards set by outside experts, and to prepare students to pass external examinations, there is no place or need for the science teacher as constructor of pedagogical or curricular knowledge. As a result, there are few resources made available to support the effort needed to engage in conventional action research.

As we've argued in this book, D-CAR and other dialogic forms of action research are not resource intensive. What it requires is the desire of practicing science teachers to set aside some time to have critical conversations about their practice. The crux of D-CAR is to provide openings for science teachers to improve their practice and educational situations, as well as to develop new understandings of them. These openings do not need to be provided by schools or districts. As a result of engaging in D-CAR, science teachers can regain the autonomy to make changes in their practice based on their own professional knowledge and improve their instruction with new pedagogy, alternative assessments, and effective classroom management methods (Yolcu & Akar-Vural, 2020). That said, a supportive school and district administration can help teachers overcome some of the restrictions of curriculum and testing and allow for a place for initiatives such as D-CAR (Whitworth & Chui, 2015).

Constraints on Science Teachers' Time

There are at least two different types of time constraints on science teachers. One is related to the need to cover a lot of content in a relatively short time in response to the enormous pressure to prepare their students for standardized exams (Dunn, 2018; Yolcu & Akar-Vural, 2020). Rather than draw from their professional knowledge or make decisions best for their students' conceptual learning (Milner, 2013), science teachers tend to teach to the test. That is, they use methods to teach answers, such as rote drilling, rather than engage their students in activities such as discussion, inquiry, and argumentation. The focus on test scores also undermines teachers' ability to make the best decisions for their students based on their learning needs. It also impedes their ability to engage in field notes and make observations while teaching (Gilbert & Smith, 2003; Kanageswari & Shok Mee, 2017).

In our research with science teachers in the climate change education project (https://climatechange.usf.edu), several of them mentioned struggling to find the time to implement new ideas in their classrooms (Feldman et al., 2021). For example, two of the teachers wanted to incorporate discussions at the end of their labs but their biggest obstacle was finding time to do so at the end of a relatively short science block. Even after successfully managing to incorporate discussions at the end of labs, they still felt rushed, and noted time was an obstacle difficult to overcome.

Another time constraint relates to the busyness of science teachers' work and personal lives. In the US and elsewhere, teaching is a full-time job that keeps teachers with students most of the school day, and then requires lesson planning and grading after the end of the day. This leaves little open time during the school day and even less after school as teaching tasks compete with family and other personal time. The result is that science teachers struggle to find time to meet with each other to engage in collaborative inquiry, or to engage in the research methods of conventional action research.

Katie saw the effects of the second type of time constraint when working with a group of teachers for her doctoral dissertation study (Laux, 2019). The science teachers struggled to find time to meet as a group to work together on their action research projects. While the original plan was to meet three or more times, the group ended up only meeting twice because of other obligations that limited their availability. In addition, two out of the four teachers ended up dropping out of the project, which left only two who were able to find the time to devote to studying how they could incorporate student voice into their practice. In addition, one of the remaining science teachers was not able to find the time to complete his data analysis. This issue, as well as lack of time to review data and write a research report, have been recognized in studies of teachers engaged in conventional action research (Gilbert & Smith, 2003; Peters, 2004; Kanageswari & Shok Mee, 2017). As a result of the heavy workload carried by science teachers, they must work longer and harder if they are to engage in conventional action research (Peters, 2004).

We have seen how D-CAR and other forms of dialogic action research can help to mitigate the effects of time constraints on science teachers. The first type of constraint we discussed above has to do with the limited time teachers have to include additional items into their classroom teaching. In conventional action research these are primarily related to the collection of data in ways similar to how it is done in the social sciences. Because D-CAR makes use of teachers' stories of practice, data collection does not need to be a highly structured process. Instead, it can rely on post hoc recollection and reflection. While there are some who would suggest this would result in inaccuracies or bias, it is possible to lessen these through the critique of their peers in their collaborative dialogues. It may also be possible to enlist a critical friend, either another teacher or an outsider, to observe some lessons.

As we noted above, the second type of time constraint has to do with lack of availability to meet, analyze data, and write up reports outside of classroom teaching time. Of course, if meeting time were made available during the school day, this constraint would be alleviated (at least for D-CAR groups made up of teachers from the same school). However, this would require a supportive administration to help facilitate the best use of limited time throughout the day. The limits on teachers' out of school time also impedes their ability to engage in conventional data analysis and reporting methods. In conventional action research, this could be viewed by teachers as "homework." If they find they don't have the time to prepare for meetings, this could lead them to dropping out of the group. This certainly seemed the case for the teachers with whom Katie worked during her dissertation work. With D-CAR what we've seen is the opposite – science teachers look forward to meeting with their colleagues to discuss their practice. This provides an intrinsic incentive for carving out the time to meet. It also eliminates the possible guilty feeling of not being prepared and letting down the rest of the group.

Difficulties in Changing One's Practice

Science teachers often face a variety of challenges when trying to implement new ideas and make changes to their practice (Lebak & Tinsley, 2010; Qablan, 2019). In general, based on the deprofessionalization of teaching discussed earlier, teachers may not have the autonomy to make decisions for their students about what they should learn and when they should learn it and, as a result, tend to be less willing to implement new ideas in their classrooms (Hodges & Tipton, 2013).

All the authors of this book have been science teachers and each of us can point to examples in our own practice in which we recognized a good teaching method but took years to implement it in our teaching. Allan tells the story of learning about a simple demonstration of electromagnetic induction. For him to use it in his physics teaching he needed to have three items. They were a 2m length of PVC tubing and the same length of copper tubing with similar diameters. The third item was a cow magnet. A cow magnet is a very strong cylindrical magnet that is used to remove bits of iron cows accidentally ingest. As it turns out, it took Allan 20 years to find where to buy that magnet and do the demonstration for his students. Clearly, it can take a lot of time and effort to change one's practice (Qablan, 2019). Rather than call this resistance to change, we acknowledge there can be good, and sometimes not so good, reasons for why change takes time.

Another issue is connected directly to the action research process itself. Teachers reported feeling uncomfortable being an agent of change or uncovering findings deemed important enough to justify doing action research in their classrooms (Kanageswari & Shok Mee, 2017). They found the open-endedness of action research and the expectations for traditional research "results" worried them throughout their initial work with action research (Slutsky et al., 2005; Suppiah Shanmugam & Mee, 2017). Teachers have reported emotions such as anxiety, frustration, uncertainty, and guilt as they struggled with learning and/or implementing conventional action research (Peters, 2004; Woodrow & Lasser, 2022).

Teaching practice is often best changed from within, starting with science teachers reflecting on their practice (Cuesta et al., 2016). Recognizing the issues in their practice can help teachers address problems and work towards solutions. Oftentimes, to make effective changes in their practice, teachers need to see things in action and have conversations with their peers (Qablan, 2019). We see the gathering together of small groups of science teachers engaged in dialogue amongst themselves as a way to overcome what gets in the way of individual teachers making changes in their teaching.

Dialogue among peers can facilitate teachers changing their practice by allowing them to engage with each other and to share experiences (Cuesta et al., 2016; Kilic, 2022). Trying out different forms of action in classrooms and reflecting together on their results allow teachers to make progress towards changing their practice. Therefore, engaging in reflective practices such as D-CAR can positively influence classroom practices and encourage teacher change (Kilic, 2022).

What About Professional Development (PD) Programs?

The good science teachers we described in Chapter 3 often seek growth opportunities such as PD programs to change or improve their practice. They do so to improve their salary, earn credit to renew their teaching certifications, allow for some career mobility, and gain new skills or knowledge. Newer science teachers are more likely to attend PD opportunities, and teachers who are more motivated to attend PD are more likely to change their teaching practice as a result (Whitworth & Chiu, 2015).

One issue with most school or district-based PD is they tend to be short-term, or even one-shot experiences. As a result, they often have little lingering effect on teachers' practice beyond the period they engaged in the PD (Kanageswari & Shok Mee, 2017), or result in no lasting or meaningful change

(Johnson et al., 2010). Another issue is that science teachers view research-based PD as secondary to teaching because it is not directly related to what they believe is important (Kanageswari & Shok Mee, 2017). Science teachers' top priorities tend to be improving their practice, and helping their students learn the knowledge and skills that will help them be productive adults and informed citizens.

Science teachers also need ongoing support and resources to implement what they learn through PD into their classrooms (Qablan, 2019). School and district personnel can provide PD for teachers that includes opportunities to receive ongoing resources and feedback (Whitworth & Chui, 2015). These leaders play a significant role in the planning and implementation of PD, as well as providing ongoing support to encourage teacher change. Involving school leaders in science education PD efforts supports teacher change by helping teachers develop professional communities, connecting teachers with resources, and encouraging changes in practice.

PD can also be transformed from a knowledge consumption process to one of knowledge construction by configuring it as practitioner research. There is ample evidence from research and teachers' own experiences that to make real changes in practice and become better educators requires continuous reflection and inquiry (Noonan, 2013). Good PD should include a focus on content, active learning, coherence in activities, be long enough in duration to make lasting change, and collective participation (Desimone, 2009; Whitworth & Chui, 2015). We believe these are all characteristics that can be addressed by D-CAR. It should also be of intrinsic value to science teachers, which is a characteristic of D-CAR. In addition, engaging in critical reflection and ongoing learning in collaborative groups through D-CAR is more likely to cause lasting changes in teaching practice (Noonan, 2013).

As stated throughout the chapter, for the successful implementation of D-CAR in schools and classrooms, support is needed from the administration and other faculty. The teachers in Katie's dissertation (Laux, 2019) encountered issues with administrative support. Both teachers who finished their action research discussed sharing the results with the school, but they thought their administration would not be supportive of a school-wide action research effort. Some of this goes back to time constraints and teachers not willing to put in extra time to engage in D-CAR with their colleagues.

One of the biggest challenges with D-CAR is maintaining the group to sustain conversations. If there is an outside facilitator, they need to help the group find a way to continue with the meetings. With the marine science teachers, only the two teachers who were working together already at the same school were able to sustain conversations about their action research. During Katie's dissertation with high school science teachers, the teachers were never able to connect on a level that allowed them to continue working together after the study. That said, the PTARG teachers continued to meet for several years after Allan moved from California for a job in Massachusetts.

Summary

This chapter addressed some of the obstacles to implementing conventional action research and how they can be mitigated through the use of D-CAR. Some of these obstacles include issues related to the deprofessionalization of teaching. Other issues are associated with time constraints teachers face when attempting to teach all required science content, as well as professional and personal commitments outside of school. Science teachers may also feel resistance to changing their practice because of how long it takes to make change or discomfort with the action research process itself. Various district or school policies may exist that prevent teachers from making teacher research a priority including the structure or focus of PD opportunities and the top-down micromanagement of the school district. Finally, science teachers may face a lack of support from administration that hinders their engagement in action research. Although the use of D-CAR is not a panacea, from our experience we believe it can ease time constraints, give support for making changes in one's practice, and provide a way to work with other science teachers that are not reliant on traditional PD models or strong support from administration.

References

Bascia, N. (2009). Teachers as professionals: Salaries, benefits and unions. In L. J. Saha & A. G. Dworkin (eds.), *International handbook of research on teachers and teaching* (pp. 481–489). Boston, MA: Springer US.

Carter Andrews, D. J., Bartell, T., & Richmond, G. (2016). Teaching in dehumanizing times: The professionalization imperative. *Journal of Teacher Education*, 67(3), 170–172. doi:10.1177/0022487116640480.

Cuesta, J., Azcarate, P., & Cardenoso, J. M. (2016). The role of reflection and collaboration in the evolution of a group of novel secondary education science teachers. *Australian Journal of Teacher Education*, 41(5), 135–152.

Desimone, L. M. (2009). Improving impact studies of teachers' professional development: Toward better conceptualizations and measures. *Educational Researcher*, 38(3), 181–199.

Dunn, A. H. (2018). Leaving a profession after it's left you: Teachers' public resignation letters as resistance amidst neoliberalism. *Teachers College Record*, 120(9), 1–34.

Etzioni, A. (1969). *The semi-professions and their organization*. Los Angeles, CA: The Free Press.

Feldman, A., Nation, M., & Laux, K. (2021). The effects of action research-based professional development on the teaching of climate science. *Educational Action Research*, 1–17.

Gilbert, S. L., & Smith, L. C. (2003). A bumpy road to action research. *Kappa Delta Pi Record*, 39(2), 80–83.

Hodges, G. W., Tippins, D., & Oliver, J. S. (2013). A study of highly qualified science teachers' career trajectory in the deep, rural south: Examining a link between deprofessionalization and teacher dissatisfaction. *School Science and Mathematics*, 113(6), 263–274. doi:10.1111/ssm.12026.

Johnson, C., Fargo, J., & Kahle, J. B. (2010). The cumulative and residual impact of a systemic reform program on teacher change and student learning of science. *School Science and Mathematics*, 110(3), 144–159.

Kanageswari, S., & Shok Mee, L. (2017). Barriers of implementing action research among Malaysian teachers. *Social Sciences and Humanities*, 25(4), 1651–1666,

Kilic, A. (2022). The impact of reflective practices on pre-service science teachers' classroom teaching practices. *Journal of Pedagogical Research*, 6(1), 152–170.

Laux, K. (2019). *Changing high school science teacher beliefs on student voice through action research*, Doctoral dissertation, University of South Florida, FL.

Lebak, K., & Tinsley, R. (2010). An inquiry and reflection be contagious? Science teachers, students, and action research. *Journal of Science Teacher Education*, 21, 953–970.

Lortie, D. C. (1975). *Schoolteacher*. Chicago, IL: The University of Chicago Press.

Manley, J. (2008). Let's fight for inquiry science! In today's climate of standardized testing, don't let inquiry science be pushed out! *Science and Children*, 45(8), 36–38.

Mansour, N. (2009). Science teachers' beliefs and practices: Issues, implications, and research agenda. *International Journal of Environmental and Science Education*, 4(1), 25–48.

Milner, H. R. (2013). Policy reforms and de-professionalization of teaching. Boulder, CO: National Education Policy Center. http://nepc.colorado.edu.

Noonan, S. J. (2013). How REAL teachers and professors learn: Threshold crossing and concepts in professional learning. *International Journal of Educational Leadership Preparation*, 8(2), 110–128.

Peters, J. (2004). Teachers engaging in action research: Challenging some assumptions. *Educational Action Research*, 12(4), 535–556.

Qablan, A. M. (2019). Effective professional development and change in practice: The case of the Queen Rania Teacher Academy science network. *EURASIA Journal of Mathematics, Science, and Technology Education*, 15(12), 1–9.

Slutsky, R., Christenson, M., Bendau, S., Covert, J., Risko, G., Dyer, J., & Johnston, M. (2005). Teacher tales of action research: Trials and triumphs. *International Electronic Journal for Leadership in Learning*, 9(4), 1–15.

Suppiah Shanmugam, S. K., & Mee, L. S. (2017). Barriers of implementing action research among Malaysian Teachers. *Pertanika Journal of Social Sciences & Humanities*, 25(4), 1651–1665.

Supovitz, J. A., & Turner, H. M. (2000). The effects of professional development on science teaching practices and classroom culture. *Journal of Research in Science Teaching*, 37(9), 963–980. doi:10.1002/1098-2736(200011)37:9<963:AID-TEA6>3.0.CO;2-0.

Whitworth, B. A., & Chiu, J. L. (2015). Professional development and teacher change: The missing leadership link. *Journal of Science Teacher Education*, 26(2), 121–137.

Woodrow, K., & Lasser, C. (2022). Fostering inclusive knowledge democracies: Layering identities and situating practices of novice teacher researchers. *Educational Action Research*, 30(5), 707–724. doi:10.1080/09650792.2020.1860104.

Yolcu, O., & Akar-Vural, R. (2020). An examination of instructional autonomy practices of science teachers. *International Journal of Educational Methodology*, 7(1), 79–94.

8 Extending the Conversation – Making D-CAR Public

Introduction

A hallmark of action research is that its products are shared with others (Eilks, 2014; Stenhouse, 1981). This chapter explores how science teachers engaging with others through dialogic collaborative action research (D-CAR) and then making it public is a knowledge production process. In addition, we will lay out how making it public leads to increasing accountability for action researchers' practice. Finally, we will demonstrate how by engaging with others outside of the D-CAR group, there is mutual learning that influences both the action researchers and the public (Robertson & Simonsen, 2012).

Importance of Sharing Conversations and Knowledge

Lawrence Stenhouse is often quoted as having defined research as "systematic inquiry made public" (Stenhouse, 1981, p. 104). Stenhouse gave several reasons for this. First, if it is not made public, then it is not open to criticism. He used criticism in the same way we do as part of what happens in a community when discussion is open, democratic, and trustful. Science teachers in D-CAR groups share what they are learning about their practice with each other, and expect to receive feedback that helps them as they inquire into their practice in order to improve it. A second reason Stenhouse gave for the need to make research public is that research is "a community effort and unpublished research is of little use to others" (p. 111). Both criticism and sharing with others can happen within the D-CAR group; however, what Stenhouse suggested goes beyond the local community to the larger community of science teachers.

When Stenhouse (1981) wrote "What Counts as Research?", the type of teacher research he and his colleagues were promoting was new, and one of his goals in the paper was to critique social science research on education as done by university researchers, and show how practitioner research ought to be considered as a legitimate form of research. To do this, he expanded what it means to make research public. A straightforward way is for science teacher researchers to share what they have learned in practitioner rather than

DOI: 10.4324/9781003307174-8

academic journals, and in presentations and workshops at their schools, in their districts, or at conferences. Of course, when Stenhouse wrote this, there was not an Internet and so he did not note all the ways teachers can disseminate their action research on the Web. Stenhouse did, however, suggest another way to make research public – through performances or actions (1981). That is, the outcomes of action research can be demonstrated through new practices that arise from it. In this way, when science teachers take actions based on their action research, it shows how what would otherwise be hypothetical becomes concrete.

Sharing for Professional, Personal, and Political Purposes of Action Research

We believe, following on Stenhouse's seminal work, all action research should be made public in some way. There are many reasons for you, as a science teacher engaged in action research, to make your work public. Because we are committed to build on the work of others before us, we organize these reasons according to Susan Noffke's descriptions of action research along the following dimensions: the professional, the personal, and/or the political (Noffke, 1997).

Sharing for Professional Purposes

Noffke (1997) wrote about three ways in which action research can serve professional purposes. One was to add to what has been called the knowledge base for teaching. Lee Shulman described the idea of this knowledge base as "a codified or codifiable aggregation of knowledge, skill, understanding, and technology, of ethics and disposition, of collective responsibility — as well as a means for representing and communicating it" (Shulman, 1987, p. 4). He included in this article a list of categories of teachers' knowledge. One was "pedagogical content knowledge" (PCK) which has become part of the lexicon of science teaching. His idea that there is a set of knowledge teachers ought to have that enables them to be successful in the classroom still resonates in the field of educational research.[1] Science teachers who engage in D-CAR could add to this knowledge base by making public what they have learned about teaching and learning while participating in their group.

Another professional purpose for action research according to Noffke (1997) is to improve the status of teaching as a profession. This would happen by science teachers being seen as not only users of knowledge but also as knowledge producers. In Chapter 7 we provided a definition for what it means for an occupation to be a profession. Other definitions also specify that professionals have mastery of a particular set of knowledge and skills, which has a research base that underlies it, and a set of moral and ethical standards (Australian Council of Professions, 2003; Cruess et al., 2004). As can be seen here, it is the connection of the mastery of knowledge and skills tied to a research base that resulted in the call for a knowledge base for teaching (Shulman, 1987).

The idea of science teachers producing new knowledge about teaching through action research that would be added to a knowledge base for teaching is laudable. However, there is still a large divide between knowledge constructed by university researchers and what is constructed by science teachers. There are multiple reasons for this, including the warrants for what counts as research in academia and where that research is published. In a way, how this plays out is the perceived lower status of teachers' action research keeps it from becoming part of the academic knowledge base for teaching, which aids in maintaining the lower status of teaching as a profession.

A third way science teacher action research can have a professional purpose is through serving professional development (PD) efforts locally or more broadly (Noffke, 1997). In recent years this has often become the domain of those teachers who are identified, either by themselves or by others, as leaders. The term "teacher leader" has different meanings in different situations, and is often left ambiguous within a particular school or district (Cheung et al., 2018). Rebecca Cheung and her colleagues (2018) describe the development of a science teacher leader profile, based on the experiences of the teachers in the school who had been designated teacher leaders. The resulting profile has four categories: collaborating with others to improve science instruction; providing resources for effective science instruction; modeling effective science instruction; and advocating in service of effective science instruction. They further divided each category into self and others. For example, collaborating with others for the self includes the science teacher leader participating in PD activities, or working with others when facilitating PD sessions. Similarly, to provide resources for the self involves keeping abreast of science news and identifying opportunities such as outside speakers, field trips, and donated materials, while sharing these resources with other science teachers. Cheung et al. (2018) found in their study the role science teacher leaders valued most important was being an advocate, even though they saw it as new, unfamiliar, and challenging. Advocating for the self includes ensuring the representation of science instruction in school governance, and analyzing the political climate of the school to support science teaching. Interestingly, it appears advocating with others is the same as advocating for the self, but in collaboration with other science teachers.

We took this digression into the nature of science teacher leadership because the way it is conceived suggests it focuses on professional purposes. Each category of teacher leadership described by Cheung et al. (2018) connects in some way to the improvement of science instruction in the school and district. If the products of action research are shared with other teachers for the purposes of the school and district as described above, it lies along the professional dimension (Noffke, 1997).

Sharing for Personal Purposes

Much of the literature on science teacher action research demonstrates one of its primary purposes is to improve teachers' practice (e.g., Capobianco, 2011;

Fazio & Melville, 2008; Lebak & Tinsley, 2010; Mitchener & Jackson, 2012). This is not surprising given that from its start, action research has been practice-based (Feldman, 2017; Hendricks, 2019), with connections to adult development, increased self-awareness, and growth in learning about practice (Elliott, 1991; Oja & Smulyan, 1989). However, there are several criticisms of this conception of action research for the improvement of one's practice. One is there is often a suggestion that action research is done by teachers as an individual activity. It is often reported this way in the practitioner journals (e.g., Martin-Dunlop, 2006; Watson & Barthlow, 2020). In addition, recently there has been a move to cast action research as an individual, problem-solving tool (Dana & Yendol-Hoppey, 2014). When action research is configured in this way, it can result in science teachers focusing on solving technical problems without regard for the larger social and political issues that may surround them. One way to reduce this effect is for action research to take place as a collaborative or group activity (Capobianco, 2007; Feldman, 1996; Goodnough, 2011; Llewellyn & van Zee, 2010; Milton-Brkich et al., 2010; Saul, 2010).

Sharing for Political Purposes

What does it mean for action research to have political purposes? The common use of the term in the US refers to the workings of governments, the engagement in political parties, or concerned with acts against a political system (Merriam-Webster Dictionary, 2022). Noffke (1997) did not provide an explicit definition; instead, she provided some examples of what she meant by political purposes. These include "creating teaching that acknowledges the voice and power of children; ... addressing particular issues such as class, race, and gender; [and] ... articulation with larger movements for social justice" (p. 334). In her discussion of the political, Noffke referred to the democratic ideal of action research:

> Whether addressed in terms of the action-research relationship, in terms of theory and practice, or in terms of blurred lines between research and advocacy, the dual agenda of interrogating the meanings of democracy and social justice at the same time as we act to alter the social situation shapes the potential of action research.
>
> (Noffke, 1997, p. 334)

Building on Noffke (1997), Allan and his colleague Mary Rearick (Rearick & Feldman, 1999) described the political purposes of action research in this way:

> action research can have political purposes, such as to critique the nature of teachers' work and workplaces and the advancement of social agendas. While doing inquiry in their classrooms, schools, and communities, action researchers can become increasingly aware of socio-economic, racial, and

gender inequalities, and of the interconnections between knowledge and power. As they identify the political ramifications of the beliefs and purposes that guide action, they become increasingly capable of directing their social action toward desired goals and of generating a language of possibility, a vision for the future, and sense of interconnectedness with others.

(p. 335)

Much of what we've discussed previously in this book could be seen as relating to the political purposes of action research. Our discussion of D-CAR as a way to deal with the wicked problems of science education resonates with Noffke's use of the term political. We've argued that a small group of science teachers can address these issues and problems locally; in addition, by making their work public they can have a greater influence in their schools and communities. While the larger effect is no way guaranteed, as we noted in Chapter 4, we share Jones' hope of the transformative effects of "quiet processes and small circles" (Religious Society of Friends, 2022, p. 24.56).

Sharing to Contribute to Knowledge Democracy

The idea of knowledge democracy responds to questions about "how knowledge is generated, by whom, how it is used, and for what purposes" (Seeley et al., 2019, p. 24). It originated in the part of the world that is sometimes referred to as the Global South, which refers broadly to the regions of Latin America, Asia, Africa, and Oceania. It is one of a family of terms, including "Third World" and "Periphery," that denote regions outside Europe and North America, mostly (though not all) low-income and often politically or culturally marginalized (Dados & Connell, 2012, p. 12).

Science teachers may be familiar with the work of Paulo Freire and his important book, *Pedagogy of the Oppressed* (1970). In this book, he called traditional teaching the "banking model of education" because it treats students as empty vessels to be filled with knowledge, which they then withdraw for tests and other assessments. He argued teaching should instead be a process of the co-construction of knowledge and understanding by the teacher and students. Science teachers may be familiar with this as constructivist pedagogy (Colburn, 2007; Hay & Barab, 2001; Tobin, 1993). However, Freire contextualized this process in the inequities in society of his home country of Brazil. His work in literacy education with oppressed people in Brazil underscored not only economic and social disparities, but also the power of the knowledge of the North over that of the South.

Orlando Fals-Borda was one of the originators of participatory action research (PAR) in Latin America (Lomeli et al., 2018). Fals-Borda's conception of PAR distinguished between the perspective of the Global North, and his vision for PAR to aid people in the Global South. He described the former as dealing with the concepts of poverty, technology, capital, growth, values, and so forth, as defined from the standpoint of rich, developed countries (where in fact the concept of development was first proposed), a discourse organised into a coherent intellectual whole for the purpose of rationalising and defending the worldwide dominance of those rich and powerful societies.

(Fals-Borda, 1987, p. 331)

For people in the Global South, according to Fals-Borda, PAR provides a way for

underdeveloped societies to articulate their own socio-political position on the basis of their own values and capacities and act accordingly to achieve their liberation from the oppressive and exploitative forms of domination imposed by opulent (capitalist) foreign powers and local consular elites and thus create a more satisfactory life for everyone.

(Fals-Borda, 1987, p. 331)

In short, what he proposed was the concept of knowledge democracy, in which the indigenous and locally constructed knowledge of the oppressed in the Global South would have the weight needed to help alleviate exploitation by the Global North.

So how does the idea of knowledge democracy apply to the sharing of the products of science teacher action research? In our discussion above about action research for professional purposes, the knowledge science teachers produce through action research is often considered having lower status than research produced by academic researchers. This is exacerbated by the push that teachers engage in "evidence-based practice" (EBP). While it makes sense that teachers use methodologies shown to be effective, the issues knowledge democracy addresses are about the type of evidence and who produces it. Cook et al. (2012) outline several characteristics of the process that determine how practices gain the label EBP. It is a systematic approach supported by research studies that "(a) are of high methodological quality, (b) use appropriate research designs that allow for assessment of effectiveness, and (c) demonstrate meaningful effect sizes such that they merit educators' trust that the practice works" (p. 497).

But who determines what are high-quality research methods, appropriate designs, or what merits educators' trust? Cook et al. (2012) appear to focus on the need to identify practices that "work," which leads them to the conclusion that what works should be determined through the use of randomized controlled experiments or quasi-experiments. This is the type of evidence that is sought for knowledge bases such as the What Works Clearinghouse (https://ies.ed.gov/ncee/wwc/). Because science teachers do not have the time or other resources to engage in this type of research, the movement to require the use of EBPs delegitimizes teachers' knowledge, as well as any type of research that could be readily conducted as part of teachers' enhanced practice. As a result, this can be looked at through a knowledge democracy lens. Overall, for those of us in the Global North, the divide between academicians and practitioners, for example university researchers and teachers, and between those who control the production and distribution of knowledge and those who are shut out of these processes due to poverty, racism, and other forms of marginalization, can be seen as the equivalent of the divide between the Global North and the Global South (Feldman & Rowell, 2019; Hong & Rowell, 2019; Katsarou & Sipitanos, 2019).

When science teachers share, and make public what they've learned through action research, they contribute to knowledge democracy. This is achieved not by going one-on-one against the power of policy makers and academicians, but through a broad coalition of teachers and their allies putting out in public the knowledge they created. Visvanathan (2009) described this as democratic imagination, "where conversation, reciprocity, translation create knowledge ... as a collaboration of memories, legacies, heritages, [and] a manifold heuristics of problem solving" that results in citizens taking power and knowledge into their hands. This is the power of the crowd, or what might be called "collective wisdom" (Landemore, 2012).

The idea of the whole being greater than its parts when it comes to the creation of knowledge, or wisdom, is often attributed to Aristotle:

> the many, who are not as individuals excellent men [sic], nevertheless can, when they have come together, be better than the few best people, not individually but collectively, just as feasts to which many contribute are better than feasts provided at one person's expense.
>
> (Aristotle, 1998, pp. 1281a1241–1281b1282)

When science teachers make public the results of their action research, they become part of a collective voice that adds credence to their findings. Because there are so many ways we are connected through Web 2.0 and other outlets, science teachers' knowledge can be distributed throughout the world of science education amongst diversely connected teachers. As Landemore (2012) noted, "viewing collective wisdom as a distributed phenomenon also precludes the view of collective wisdom as necessarily involving a central authority" (p. 8). That is, the collective wisdom of science teachers' action research adds to knowledge democracy, and demonstrates, for example, that teaching practices can be evidence-based through teachers' collective wisdom, rather than relying on experiments conducted by the university researchers who are recognized in the "Global North" as the authorities.

Methods of Sharing

So far in this chapter we have presented several arguments as to why it is important for science teachers to share what they've learned through their engagement in action research. In the remainder of the chapter we discuss some of the ways this can be done. We purposefully begin with the types of sharing science teachers often use in their practice. Some of them have been described as part of the role of teacher leaders. However, to us, most are ways good teachers normally collaborate with their colleagues.

We also want to note that many genres can be used for sharing. Science teachers will be most familiar with the traditional format of a scientific report with headings such as Introduction, Methods and Materials, Results, and Discussion (The Writing Center, 2022). They may also have been taught that research reports should not be written in the first person (use of "I" or "we"). Sometimes this is referred to as using the third person, but that's not quite accurate. The style has been to use the passive voice, which really doesn't have a "person." For example, a scientific report on coastline ecology may use phrasing like "samples were collected from locations 10m apart along the shoreline." Notice there is no one identified as doing the sampling. Written reports of action research are not restricted to these conventions for scientific writing. In fact, there has been a shift to more fluid writing in science, and to the use of both the first person and the active voice. This would result in the example above being written like this: "We collected the samples from locations 10m apart along the shoreline."

Reports of action research are also not restricted to written formats. For example, in the book *Teachers Investigate their Work* (Feldman et al., 2018) the authors describe how action research can be reported through arts-based forms like art installations, exhibits, performances, video and photography, and other graphic forms. There are also creative ways to present your work to a group, for example, PechaKucha presentations or the use of software such as Prezi. A PechaKucha presentation consists of 20 images that are each on the screen for 20 seconds. The images are advanced automatically and presenters speak as the images change. The total presentation lasts 400 seconds, which is less than seven minutes (https://www.pechakucha.com). Prezi is a hypermedia presentation software. It is a non-linear way of presenting information that allows the presenter to jump in and around the presentation, which enables you to tell and share your research in a fluid manner. All of these examples are in addition to more traditional ways to share your work including posters, workshops, and print and non-print media. However, rather than provide details on how to use the various creative forms of representation of research, which can be readily found on the Internet, our focus is to describe and discuss the venues for reporting action research.

Sharing Within the D-CAR Group

The most immediate way to share the results of action research is within the D-CAR group, because it is collaborative and engages science teachers in conversation with each other. In D-CAR, the continuing exchange of ideas, observations, conclusions, and so on, is how knowledge is constructed and shared within the group. It also provides the opportunity to test out ideas and methods in different educational situations by different teachers. In doing so, it helps to counter the criticism that teachers' research does not have enough of an evidentiary base for it to be considered valid.

Sharing With Local Colleagues

It also makes sense for science teachers to make use of formal and informal ways to share with colleagues within their departments, schools, and school districts. Science teachers who worked with us have made presentations about their action research in their science departments and to colleagues in school-based professional learning communities (PLCs). These are low stakes venues in which there usually already exists trust among the groups' members, which encourages open, non-critical exchanges.

Presentations and Workshops

The world of science teaching offers many venues for presenting the outcomes of teachers' action research. Many countries have national science teacher associations. In the US it is the National Science Teachers Association (NSTA) (https://www.nsta.org), in the UK the Association for Science Education (https://www.ase.org.uk/), and in Saudi Arabia the Saudi Scientific Association for Teachers (SSAT) (https://ssat.kku.edu.sa). ICASE, the International Council of Associations for Science Education (https://www.icaseonline.net), maintains a list of its member associations from all over the world. Typically these national associations have yearly conferences or meetings at which science teachers make presentations related to their teaching methods. Often there are also regional associations. For example, in Florida, where two of us live, there is the Florida Association of Science Teachers (https://fastscience. wildapricot.org/), which has a yearly conference. In Iowa, where Katie lives, there is the Iowa Academy of Science (http://www.iowaacademyofscience. wildapricot.org/), which publishes the Iowa Science Teachers Journal (http s://scholarworks.uni.edu/istj/). There are even more groups, like the Hillsborough Association of Elementary Science Teachers (HAEST) (https://www.facebook.com/profile.php?id=100016460464545), which serves the Tampa Bay region. These venues typically have a variety of presentation options including traditional, roundtables, posters, workshops, and possibly ones that are creative and interactive. In traditional presentations, the presenter is in front of an audience and gives an overview of the action research, usually with the use of PowerPoint or other presentation apps. Roundtables are just that: the opportunity to sit at a small table with peers to present and discuss your work. Poster presentations are usually part of a large room of posters in which the audience walks from poster to poster, getting a brief description of the work from the presenter, and asking follow-up questions. Workshops are longer sessions used to teach audience members how to engage with or in what you learned from your action research. Presentations can also be in the form of multimedia presentations, art installations, and even performance (e.g., dance, music, theater).

Action Research Networks

The good news for those who promote and engage in action research is there are action research networks all over the world. One of the oldest is the Collaborative Action Research Network (CARN), which was founded in 1976 in the UK (https://www.carn.org.uk). Most of CARN's activities are in Europe. It has an annual conference and sponsors several publications: the academic journal *Educational Action Research* (https://www.tandfonline.com/journals/reac20); the CARN Bulletin (https://www.carn.org.uk/resources/carn-bulletins/), which features papers presented at CARN conferences; and a new publication, *CARN Praxis* (https://www.carn.org.uk/resources/carn-praxis/), that is devoted to the publication of action research by practitioners and new researchers. CARN also sponsors Study Days, which are locally sponsored and focus on ideas that are important to them in relation to their practice, their context, and their values. For example, one was held in summer 2022 sponsored by the Portuguese network, Estreiadiálogos (https://www.estreiadialogos.com).

The Action Research Network of the Americas (ARNA) was established in 2012 to serve the action research communities in north and south America (https://arnawebsite.org). As such, it is committed to using all the major languages of the Americas including English, French, Spanish, and Portuguese, in addition to indigenous languages. As part of its 2017 conference in Cartagena, Colombia, it sponsored the "1st Global Assembly for Knowledge Democracy."

The Action Learning, Action Research Association (ALARA) was founded in 1989 in Brisbane, Australia (https://www.alarassociation.org/). Its homepage describes ALARA as a "global network of programs, institutions, professionals, and people interested in using action learning and action research to generate collaborative learning, training, research and action to transform workplaces, schools, colleges, universities, communities, voluntary organisations, governments and businesses." It holds both yearly conferences and world congresses.

There are many national and regional action research networks. These include, for example, the Network for Educational Action Research in Ireland (NEARI) (http://www.eari.ie/), the Society for Participatory Research in ASIA (PRIA) (https://pria.org/), the Pan-Canadian Coalition on Community Based Research (https://www.communityresearchcanada.ca/), and the Nordic Network for Action Reseach (https://www.gu.se/pedagogik-specialpedagogik/nordiskt-natverk-for-aktionsforskning), among others. There is also Action Research to Innovate Science Teaching (ARTIST) (http://www.erasmus-artist.eu/index.html). ARTIST has its origin in action research projects funded by the ERASMUS+ Programme of the European Union. Its partners include institutions in Germany, Austria, Ireland, Turkey, and the Philippines. It sponsors the online journal, *The Journal of Action Research and Innovation in Science Education* (https://www.arisejournal.com/).

We began this section by noting the existence of these networks is good news. The bad news is while they are all open to practitioners, most of the presentations at their conferences and in their journals are made by university researchers who have as their primary interest the study of action research. There are also presentations and articles that reflect the university researchers' roles as practitioners, typically as instructors or facilitators of action research. Although this appears to be problematic, science teacher action researchers are generally more interested in sharing what they've learned with other science teachers. This being the case, with their predominantly university researcher focus, these action research networks might not be the best venues for sharing and learning about the teaching of science.

Publishing in Journals

There are many journals related to action research; these are either open access or require a membership or subscription. Some of these journals are more researcher-focused such as *Educational Action Research* (EAR) (https://www.tandfonline.com/journals/reac20) or *Action Research* (https://journals.sagepub.com/home/arj). Others are more practitioner-focused and tend to be more appropriate for educators who are practicing in the field. These journals are often specific to certain content areas. For example, Allan, Molly, and Katie published an article in *The Science Teacher* with one of the marine science teachers who participated in the action research group; it can be accessed through the National Science Teaching Association (NSTA) website (https://www.nsta.org). This allowed the teacher, Amy Dobson, to disseminate the information she learned through her action research related to inquiry.

Publication on the Internet including Web 2.0

Another method of sharing information is through publishing online through Web 2.0 tools. Examples of these tools include wikis, blogs, Twitter, Facebook, Instagram, and Tiktok. Publishing through these tools allows science teacher action researchers to reach a wide audience. There are a number of additional benefits including facilitating collaboration and interaction, offering immediate feedback, and opening opportunities for the development of professional communities (Andersen & Matkins, 2011; Çetin et al., 2019; Childers & Hite, 2022; Stinson, 2015; Wall & Anderson, 2015). In addition, these tools enhance the potential of engaging other science teachers around the world to create communities of practice, decreasing isolation, expanding self-esteem and self-efficacy, supporting the exchange of ideas and knowledge, and encouraging teaching and learning innovation (Duncan-Howell, 2010; The National Educational Technology Plan, 2010).

In the previous sections of this chapter we supplied some websites that could be appropriate for publishing the work of science teacher action researchers. Others include Teachers Pay Teachers (https://www.teacherspayteachers.com), Teach

Engineering (https://www.teachengineering.org), the *Journal of Teacher Action Research* (http://www.practicalteacherresearch.com), and *Networks: An Online Journal for Teacher Research* (https://newprairiepress.org/networks). There are many others out there on the Internet, and there will undoubtedly be many more possibilities as the Internet changes and grows.

Summary

In this chapter our goals were to provide information about why it is important for science teachers to share the results of their action research studies. Following up on the framework developed by Noffke (1997), we examined professional, personal, and political reasons for doing so. The professional reasons include adding to the knowledge base of science teaching, for example codifying PCK; to improve the status of teaching by demonstrating that science teachers can produce new knowledge about teaching and learning; and to use their results to inform PD efforts locally or more broadly. For the most part the personal reasons for science teachers have for engaging in action research and sharing their results is to improve their practice and that of other science teachers. Finally, the political reasons are to deal with wicked problems and to contribute to knowledge democracy. In the remainder of the chapter we provided suggestions for how to reach other educators through different venues and platforms. In the next chapter we offer some examples of science teacher action research that used dialogic or conversational modes of research.

Note

1 At the time of our writing this chapter, an ERIC search for the phrase "pedagogical content knowledge" in article titles found over 40 published in 2021. For the most part, these articles described the pedagogical content knowledge found in the study of teachers of varying subjects and levels.

References

Andersen, L., & Matkins, J. J. (2011). Web 2.0 tools and the reflections of preservice secondary science teachers. *Journal of Digital Learning in Teacher Education*, 28(1), 27–38. doi:10.1080/21532974.2011.10784677.

Aristotle (1998). *Politics* (translated by C. D. C. Reeve). Indianapolis, IN: Hackett Press.

Australian Council of Professions (2003). What is a profession? Deakin, ACT: Australian Council of Professions. Retrieved March 11 from https://www.professions.org.au/what-is-a-professional/.

Capobianco, B. M. (2007). Science teachers' attempts at integrating feminist pedagogy through collaborative action research. *Journal of Research in Science Teaching*, 44(1), 1–32. doi:10.1002/tea.20120.

Capobianco, B. M. (2011). Exploring a science teacher's uncertainty with integrating engineering design: An action research study. *Journal of Science Teacher Education*, 22(7), 645–660. doi:10.1007/s10972-010-9203-2.

Çetin, N. M., Telli, E., Daghan, G., & Akkoyunlu, B. (2019). Determining reflectivity levels of prospective teachers through blogs. *International Online Journal of Education and Teaching*, 6(3), 582–596.

Cheung, R., Reinhardt, T., Stone, E., & Little, J. W. (2018). Defining teacher leadership: A framework. *Phi Delta Kappan*, 100(3), 38–44.

Childers, G., & Hite, R. (2022). The role of emerging technologies in science teacher preparation. In J. A. Luft & M. G. Jones (eds.), *Handbook of research on science teacher education* (pp. 218–230). New York and Abingdon, UK: Routledge.

Colburn, A. (2007). Constructivism and conceptual change, part II. *The Science Teacher*, 74(8), 14.

Cook, B. G., Smith, G. J., & Tankersley, M. (2012). Evidence-based practices in education. In K. R. Harris, S. Graham, T. Urdan, C. B. McCormick, G. M. Sinatra, & J. Sweller (eds.), *APA educational psychology handbook, Vol 1: Theories, constructs, and critical issues* (pp. 495–527). Washington, DC: American Psychological Association. doi:10.1037/13273-017.

Cruess, S. R., Johnston, S., & Cruess, R. L. (2004). "Profession": A working definition for medical educators. *Teaching and Learning in Medicine*, 16(1), 74–76. doi:10.1207/s15328015tlm1601_15.

Dados, N., & Connell, R. (2012). The Global South. *Contexts*, 11(1), 12–13. doi:10.1177/1536504212436479.

Dana, N. F., & Yendol-Hoppey, D. (2014). *The reflective educator's guide to classroom research: Learning to teach and teaching to learn through practitioner inquiry.* Thousand Oaks, CA: Corwin Press.

Duncan-Howell, J. (2010). Teachers making connections: Online communities as a source of professional learning. *British Journal of Educational Technology*, 41(2), 324–340.

Eilks, I. (2014). Action research in science education: From a general justification to a specific model in practice. In T. Stern, A. Townsend, F. Rauch, & A. Schuster (eds.), *Action research, innovation and change: International perspectives across disciplines* (pp. 156–176). Oxford, UK: Routledge.

Elliott, J. (1991). *Action research for educational change.* Buckingham, UK: Open University Press.

Fals-Borda, O. (1987). The application of participatory action-research in Latin America. *International Sociology*, 2(4), 329–347. doi:10.1177/026858098700200401.

Fazio, X., & Melville, W. (2008). Science teacher development through collaborative action research. *Teacher Development*, 12(3), 193–209. doi:10.1080/13664530802259222.

Feldman, A. (1996). Enhancing the practice of physics teachers: Mechanisms for the generation and sharing of knowledge and understanding in collaborative action research. *Journal of Research in Science Teaching*, 33(5), 513–540.

Feldman, A. (2017). An emergent history of educational action research in the English-speaking world. In L. L. Rowell, C. D. Bruce, J. M. Shosh, & M. M. Riel (eds.), *The Palgrave international handbook of action research* (pp. 125–145). Springer.

Feldman, A., & Rowell, L. (2019). Knowledge democracy and action research – an exchange. *Educational Action Research*, 27(3), 335–346. doi:10.1080/09650792.2019.1618624.

Feldman, A., Altrichter, H., Posch, P., & Somekh, B. (2018). *Teachers investigate their work: An introduction to action research across the professions* (3rd edition). New York and Abingdon, UK: Routledge.

Freire, P. (1970). *Pedagogy of the oppressed.* New York: Continuum.

Goodnough, K. (2011). *Taking action in science classrooms through collaborative action research a guide for educators.* Rotterdam: Sense Publishers.

Hay, K. E., & Barab, S. A. (2001). Constructivism in practice: A comparison and contrast of apprenticeship and constructionist learning environments. *The Journal of the Learning Sciences*, 10(3), 281–322. doi:10.1207/S15327809JLS1003_3.

Hendricks, C. C. (2019). History of action research in education. In C. A. Mertler (ed.), *The Wiley handbook of action research in education* (pp. 29–51). New York: John Wiley & Sons. doi:10.1002/9781119399490.ch2.

Hong, E., & Rowell, L. (2019). Challenging knowledge monopoly in education in the U.S. through democratizing knowledge production and dissemination. *Educational Action Research*, 27(1), 125–143. doi:10.1080/09650792.2018.1534694.

Katsarou, E., & Sipitanos, K. (2019). Contemporary school knowledge democracy: Possible meanings, promising perspectives and necessary prerequisites. *Educational Action Research*, 27(1), 108–124. doi:10.1080/09650792.2018.1564688.

Landemore, H. (2012). Collective wisdom: Old and new. In H. Landemore & J. Elster (eds.), *Collective wisdom: Principles and mechanisms* (pp. 1–20). Cambridge: Cambridge University Press. doi:10.1017/CBO9780511846427.001.

Lebak, K., & Tinsley, R. (2010). Can inquiry and reflection be contagious? Science teachers, students, and action research. *Journal of Science Teacher Education*, 21(8), 953–970. doi:10.1007/s10972-010-9216-x.

Llewellyn, D., & van Zee, E. (2010). Action research: Expanding the role of classroom teachers to inquirers and researchers. *Science Scope*, 34(1), 10.

Lomeli, R., Dilean, J., & Rappaport, J. (2018). Imagining Latin American social science from the Global South: Orlando Fals Borda and participatory action research. *Latin American Research Review*, 53, 597–612. doi:10.25222/larr.164.

Martin-Dunlop, C. (2006). Science learning environments and action research. *Science Scope*, 30(1), 44–47.

Merriam-Webster Dictionary (2022). Political. Retrieved May 22 from https://www.merriam-webster.com/dictionary/political https://www.merriam-webster.com/dictionary/political.

Milton-Brkich, K. L., Shumbera, K., & Beran, B. (2010). Action research. *Science and Children*, 47(9), 47.

Mitchener, C. P., & Jackson, W. M. (2012). Learning from action research about science teacher preparation. *Journal of Science Teacher Education*, 23(1), 45–64. doi:10.1007/s10972-011-9261-0.

Noffke, S. E. (1997). Professional, personal, and political dimensions of action research. *Review of Research in Education*, 22, 305–343. doi:10.3102/0091732X022001305.

Oja, S., & Smulyan, L. (1989). *Collaborative action research: A developmental approach*. London: Falmer Press.

Rearick, M., & Feldman, A. (1999). Orientations, product, reflections: A framework for understanding action research. *Teaching and Teacher Education*, 15(4), 333–350. doi:10.1016/S0742-051X(98)00053-5.

Religious Society of Friends (2022). *Quaker faith & practice* (5th edition). London: Religious Society of Friends (Quakers). https://qfp.quaker.org.uk/passage/24-56/.

Saul, W. (2010). Making the case for action research. *Science Scope*, 34(1), 24–29.

Seeley, J., McAteer, M., Osorio Sánchez, C., & Kenfield, Y. (2019). Creating a space for global dialogue on knowledge democracy: Experiences from the inaugural global assembly for knowledge democracy. *Educational Action Research*, 27(1), 22–39. doi:10.1080/09650792.2018.1552170.

Shulman, L. (1987). Knowledge and teaching: Foundations of the new reform. *Harvard Educational Review*, 57(1), 1–22. doi:10.17763/haer.57.1.j463w79r56455411.

Stenhouse, L. (1981). What counts as research? *British Journal of Educational Studies*, 29(2), 103–114.

Stinson, A. (2015). Exploring 8th grade middle school science teachers' use of Web 2.0 tools. *Alabama Journal of Educational Leadership*, 2, 26–35.

The National Educational Technology Plan (2010). *Transforming American education: Learning powered by technology: National Educational Technology Plan 2010*. Washington, DC: US Department of Education, Office of Educational Technology.

The Writing Center (2022). *Scientific reports*. Chapel Hill, NC: University of North Carolina at Chapel Hill. Retrieved June 6 from https://writingcenter.unc.edu/tips-and-tools/scientific-reports/.

Tobin, K. G. (ed.). (1993). *The practice of constructivism in science education*. Washington, DC: AAAS Press.

Visvanathan, S. (2009, June 1). The search for cognitive justice. *The Monthly Symposium*. http://www.india-seminar.com/2009/597/597_shiv_visvanathan.htm.

Wall , S. D., & Anderson, J. (2015). Peer communication through blogging. *Contemporary Issues in Technology and Teacher Education (CITE Journal)*, 15(4), 514–540.

Watson, S. B., & Barthlow, M. J. (2020). Action research for science teachers. *Science Teacher*, 87(6), 26–29. https://search.ebscohost.com/login.aspx?direct=true&db=eue&AN=141707533&site=ehost-live.

9 Cases of D-CAR

Introduction

In the preceding chapters we used examples from our work to present and explain the different aspects of dialogic collaborative action research (D-CAR). In this chapter we provide examples of other action research studies that have used conversations and dialogues as a research method. The literature on action research in science education has little in the way of explicit examples of science teachers engaged in D-CAR. However, we found examples indicating that, although the way in which action research is defined in the articles suggests the use of conventional methods, the description of what happened in the groups is of mostly dialogical processes. We begin with three examples that address important issues in science education – the use of technology; the teaching of inquiry and the nature of science; and the encouragement of science teachers to take an inquiry stance toward their practice. We found few examples that focused on wicked problems and described dialogical processes among the science teachers. The six examples span four decades, from the 1990s to the 2020s. They are the teaching of controversial issues, dissemination of innovative curricula, the need to engage a wide range of stakeholders, using feminist pedagogy, including Indigenous knowledge in science classes, self-organized science teacher communities in response to neoliberal policies, and including equity in STEM education.

Action Research to Address Non-Wicked Problems in Science Education

Science Teachers Use of Technology

In our first example Karthigeyan Subramaniam, a university researcher, collaborated with five 10th grade science teachers in Texas on a project to examine how the teachers' roles changed as they incorporated computer technology into their practice (2010). Subramaniam used a definition of collaborative action research that draws on the work of Capobianco (2007), Feldman and Capobianco (2008), Fazio and Melville (2008), and Nelson (2009), among others, and is similar to what we articulated in Chapter 3: "Collaborative action research is an approach

DOI: 10.4324/9781003307174-9

that supports teachers as researchers coming together to explore, examine, and negotiate issues concerning science instruction" (Subramaniam, 2010, p. 938). He added that this approach to action research aligns with what he sees as one of its fundamental aims, which is for teachers to improve their teaching through the construction of knowledge, transformation of learning, and by being empowered.

The five science teachers in the group investigated their practice by engaging in autobiographical reflection using narratives and metaphors, and collaborative reflection in their group meetings (Rearick & Feldman, 1999; Subramaniam, 2010). Their decision to examine their use of technology was influenced by their school's focus on preparing students for state-mandated examinations and the availability of computers and Internet in all of their classrooms. Subramaniam organized the action research into several components. He began by helping the teachers develop individual research questions and action plans. The second component took place after the teachers taught a lesson using computer technology. He asked the teachers to complete three tasks: 1) to reflect on their teaching role during the lesson and write a metaphorical statement (Tobin & Tippins, 1996); 2) to write a narrative that explains their metaphors; and 3) to relate their narratives to the phrase "the teacher as …" (Tobin & Tippins, 1996). The third component consisted of meetings of the science teachers with Subramaniam that he organized using questions like:

> (a) What change do you see in your teaching role when teaching with computer technology? (b) Are there any similarities and differences in your findings? and (c) Collectively, how would you describe the change in your teaching role when teaching with computer technology?
>
> (Subramaniam, 2010, p. 942)

In discussions science teachers talked about how their roles were more than management of the technology. Instead they used it to enhance student learning through visualization to help students construct their understandings of scientific concepts, and as a way for students to use computers as an interactive tool to manipulate variables and test ideas.

Subramaniam (2010) concluded that autobiographical and collaborative reflection by the teachers on their practice helped them to understand their roles as diversified and expanded when using computer technology. The collaborative sharing of their action research experiences helped them to negotiate their new roles and how they related to students' learning of science content. In addition, they created new instructional knowledge based on each other's shared perspectives. Because the teachers were engaged in their action research collaboratively, we see their discussions as a form of D-CAR.

Scientific Inquiry and the Nature of Science

Our second example is from Ontario, Canada. Xavier Fazio and Wayne Melville (2008) engaged four science teachers in action research. The teachers were recruited from a master's level science education course to participate in an action research group to explore their use of scientific inquiry (SI) and the nature of science (NOS). Although the authors state each of the teachers engaged in individual action research projects – for example, "Facilitating Student Learning of the Theory-Laden and Tentative Aspects of Science, Using Historical and Philosophical Perspectives" and "Supporting and Assessing Students' Scientific Inquiry Skills During the Development of Science Fair Projects" (Fazio, 2009) – Fazio and Melville do not describe what the teachers did for those projects. The two articles instead focus on what the science teachers did when they came together for their 12, two-hour collaborative bi-weekly meetings. The purpose of the meetings was for the teachers along with Fazio, who was the facilitator, to "share ideas, critically examine and reflect upon [their] views and current practices and to collaboratively reflect on the processes and products of the individual action research projects" (Fazio & Melville, 2008, p. 196). They did this by sharing anecdotes of their teaching, the generation and sharing of curriculum materials, getting feedback from the others about the plans and actions, and exploring resources for curriculum development.

The science teachers spoke about the importance of the social benefits of participating in the collaborative action research group in interviews with Fazio and Melville (2008). This included both the sharing of ideas and resources, and their public and critical reflection on scientific inquiry, the nature of science, and on one another's teaching practices. Fazio and Melville saw that collaborative reflection in the group on the individual projects led to broader reflections as the teachers helped each other through solving problems of science education. They conclude the article with this model of action research: practice → theory → re-formed practice → reformed theory → practice → (reiteration of practice), which they see as the process of theorizing with teachers, as described by McNiff (2006). For us, this is another example of D-CAR because of the collaboration among the science teachers and Fazio and Melville, and the dialogical sharing of ideas and reflection in the group meetings.

Taking an Inquiry Stance

In our third example of action research to address non-wicked problems in science education, Tamara Nelson (2009) looked at the effects of science and mathematics teachers' participation in professional learning communities (PLCs). Proponents of PLCs, including Nelson, describe them as consisting of communities of teachers who engage in inquiry, rely on the use of data, recognize the cultures of schools, and often have the goal to increase equity (Cochran-Smith & Lytle, 2009). However, as we noted in Chapter 5, PLC teachers have not always had the opportunity to structure their PLCs so that they have these characteristics.

The PLCs studied by Nelson (2009) were established as part of a project at Washington State University Vancouver and funded by the state Office of the

Superintendent of Public Instruction. They were part of a three-year project that included six school districts. Nine PLCs were followed as part of her larger study. During the second year, three of the PLCs, which provided recordings of their meetings, were the focus of Nelson's article. The participants in two of the PLCs taught physical science, while the third was a mix of science and mathematics teachers. A central tenet of the project was for the teachers to take an inquiry stance as they investigated their work. Marilyn Cochran-Smith and Susan Lytle (2009) describe teachers who take an inquiry stance as working within communities to "generate local knowledge, envision and theorize their practice, and interpret and interrogate the theory and research of others" (Cochran-Smith & Lytle, 2009, p. 289). These communities are both social and political as the teachers make problematic issues like the arrangements of schooling, how knowledge is constructed, evaluated, and used, and their roles as change agents.

The teachers in each of the PLCs identified a problem of practice they wanted to address, including improving students' abilities to plan science investigations and draw conclusions from them; improving students' command of mathematical and scientific language; and improving students' abilities to write scientific conclusions. Teachers in the three PLCs worked together on collective activities related to writing and implementing instructional materials, and developing and administering pre/posttests. However, little of this is discussed by Nelson (2009). In fact, she noted that in only one of the nine PLCs in the larger study did the teachers engage in inquiry cycles typical of conventional action research. Instead, her focus was on the collaborative conversations the teachers engaged in during their PLC meetings. These conversations primarily focused on three areas:

> (1) collectively planning and implementing activities; (2) raising questions about teaching, learning, curriculum, and disciplinary goals; and (3) reflecting on both the impact of their actions on student learning as well as what to do about their still existing questions.
>
> (Nelson, 2009, p. 557)

Nelson concluded with the statement that the three PLCs illustrated the importance of teachers engaging dialogically with one another. In addition, she argued sustained dialogue is essential to PLCs in which the teachers take an inquiry stance, so they contribute to transformations in teachers' knowledge and understanding that have positive impacts on their teaching and their students' learning.

Action Research to Address Wicked Problems in Science Education

We now turn to examples of how science teachers have engaged in D-CAR to address wicked educational problems. As we noted above, we found few examples in the literature of science teacher action research that used dialogic methods and addressed wicked problems. In order to provide readers with examples that focus on a wide variety of wicked problems that science teachers may want to address, some of the cases below are not as recent as we would have liked. However, all the cases focus on wicked problems that are still relevant to science teachers.

Engaging with Stem Cell Research in High School Biology

In Chapter 4 we described two types of wicked problems in science education. The first type were problems related to science, technology, or engineering issues, while the second were related to broader educational issues. In this example, Bev France and her colleagues (2012) worked with science teachers in New Zealand who wrestled with the teaching of stem cell research. Stem cell research is an example of a controversial topic in science. In Chapter 4 we discussed the nature of these types of topics and what makes them controversial. In particular, the teaching of different aspects of biotechnology, which includes genetic testing, genetically modified organisms, as well as stem cell research, raises political, social, and economic concerns (Oulton et al., 2004). This was the case in New Zealand where six teachers of senior biology collaborated in action research with France and her colleagues to help students to cross cultural borders to discuss controversial topics, like stem cell research, which were outside of their life worlds.

France et al. (2012) engaged the six teachers in collaborative action research that had three components: a set of resources on current stem cell research; two teaching strategies to provide a framework for discussing the topic in their classes; and "four 2 [hour] professional development sessions that enabled the participants to discuss, evaluate, and develop their responses to these resources" (France et al., 2012, p. 806). From the description of the sessions, it appears the teachers engaged in a dialogic form of action research. In the first two sessions the teachers examined and discussed the resources and teaching strategies relative to their teaching situations. In the third session they presented how they planned to address the topic of stem cell research in their classes. The final session was devoted to the teachers explaining what they did, their evaluation of the lessons, and how they adapted the provided resources and strategies to their situations. These sessions provided the teachers with the collaborative and communal reflective space (Rearick & Feldman, 1999) to identify and cross the knowledge, language, and social barriers their students faced. As France et al. (2012) noted, these barriers are often hidden to teachers. They found when the science teachers engaged in dialogue about their practice situations in the four sessions, it "made visible the micro cultures of school, church and family that their students experienced" (France et al., 2012, p. 812). These included the language barriers faced by students who were English language learners, the traditional expectations placed on the Polynesian girls, and religious beliefs, especially in the classes in parochial schools.

Curriculum Dissemination

Many educators might not think of curriculum dissemination as a wicked educational problem. However, it often is as we can see in this example from South Africa of science teacher action research for the development of curriculum for environmental education. R. B. O'Donoghue and C. McNaught (1991), who work with the Natal Parks Board and University of Natal, recognized the traditional center–periphery model (CPM) of curriculum development was not working in their situation. They described CPM as a "scientific approach," which relies on external, rational, and objective research to develop the curriculum, and is then distributed to be used by teachers. As they found, CPM in general has failed to achieve more than superficial and short-term changes. This is what they saw in the Action Ecology project, which was an attempt to use CPM to address problems they saw in their school visits and fieldwork experiences at the Natal Parks. They also came to realize there were competing approaches to environmental education, as well as lack of resources and syllabus constraints that limited how the externally developed materials were being used. In addition, they came to envision environmental issues as a combination of political, social, economic, and bio-physical factors. In short, they came to understand environmental education as a wicked educational problem.

O'Donoghue and McNaught (1991), based on the above, rejected the CPM and replaced it with collaborative problem solving through action research. This consisted of "a sustained dialogue [among teachers] around the prevailing science curriculum, local environmental issues and everyday classroom activities [that] fostered reconstructive change at local level" (O'Donoghue & McNaught, 1991, p. 391), supported by external support services. They convened two groups of science teachers from isolated rural schools and met once or twice a month for seven to eight months. Each group had a chairperson who was selected by the teachers, and was supported by a researcher from one of the Natal environmental education field centers. The groups, including the outside researcher, worked as a collaborative team. In addition, the two groups had the opportunity to exchange ideas. O'Donoghue and McNaught saw the groups to be engaged in an exciting and creative manner to identify problems relative to their teaching of environmental education and develop resources to address them. The teachers produced resources, including color charts, fieldwork reference books, and worksheets, which were locally published and made available to other teachers in a database.

To O'Donoghue and McNaught (1991), the research design that arose from this project was an example of science teachers becoming "a critical community of scientists engaged in the reconstructive enquiry of the way they see and act in the world" (O'Donoghue & McNaught, 1991, p. 401). Referring to Ira Shor and Paolo Freire (1987), they note "reflective dialogic processes in intersubjective situations are central both in the construction and the transformation of reality [and] the centrality of dialogue in emancipatory change" (O'Donoghue & McNaught, 1991, p. 401). It should be clear from the prevalence of the use of dialogue in the groups, this again is an example of D-CAR.

Re-Imagining the Elements of Science, Technology, and Society (STS) Education

In 1982 the US National Science Teachers Association (NSTA) published a position paper titled "Science-Technology-Society: Science Education for the 1980s" (Berkheimer et al., 1983).[1] In the position statement, the authors offer this declaration:

> The goal of science education during the 1980s is to develop scientifically literate individuals who understand how science, technology, and society influence one another and who are able to use this knowledge in their everyday decision-making. The scientifically literate person has a substantial knowledge base of facts, concepts, conceptual networks, and process skills which enable the individual to continue to learn and think logically. This individual both appreciates the value of science and technology in society and understands their limitations.
>
> (Berkheimer et al., 1983, p. 16)

Although science educators had been discussing the idea of science–technology–society (STS) since the 1970s, the publication of this statement led to major efforts in the US and elsewhere to develop STS curriculum materials and offer professional development (PD) to teachers to implement the materials (Kumar & Berlin, 1993). That said, as with many reform efforts in education, there was little impact on classroom teaching. A reason for the lack of impact was the preponderance of the use of the CPM of curriculum change. This model, which treats science teachers as passive recipients of knowledge, is rarely effective. As we saw in the previous example, dialogic forms of action research change the roles of science teachers from knowledge receivers to knowledge producers.

In this example, Erminia Pedretti (1996) reported on her facilitation of a group of six science teachers engaged in action research on teaching STS in the Toronto, CA area. She selected action research as a form of PD because, if STS curricula are to be effective, groups of teachers who know the children, locality, and school environment need to be brought together "in a critical but supportive environment ... [beginning] with reflection on their current practice, proceeding through critical consideration of alternatives, and then to deciding on, implementing and evaluating curriculum actions" (Pedretti, 1996, p. 432). In action research, teachers have the opportunity to do this as they articulate, analyze, critique, and compare their ideas with others in a trusting and supportive group.

The action research group met every two to three weeks during the 1992–93 academic year. During that year, the science teachers kept individual journals and collaborated with one another in reflecting on STS theories and practices, and their own beliefs and practices. They also set long-term goals, developed and implemented STS curriculum units, reflected on their implementation, and modified the units. An important aspect of their group work was to come to a collective vision of STS education. As they wrestled with this, tensions and differences in values and beliefs surfaced. However, as Pedretti (1996) noted, these tensions were a valuable part of the discourse as the group struggled toward a shared understanding of STS education. Through this dialogical process they agreed on four crucial elements of STS education: critical social reconstruction, decision-making, action, and sustainability. Continued discussion, what Pedretti describes as an intense exploration of STS education over the course of months of hard work, collaboration, and critical examination of STS, led them to construct a model of STS education in which the interactions of science, technology, society, and the environment (STSE) leads to decision-making and taking action. Pedretti concluded action research can provide valuable collaboration among teachers that overcomes isolation by establishing links with other teachers and with researchers like herself. It provided this group of science teachers the opportunity to engage in dialogue about STS education in their own educational situations while simultaneously being able to share their interests, concerns, and knowledge with the others in a critical and supportive forum.

Integrating Feminist Pedagogy Through Action Research

The way in which gender plays out in science classrooms and in the science, technology, engineering, and math (STEM) disciplines is a wicked problem. In 2000, Brenda Capobianco convened an action research group of 11 high school science teachers in Massachusetts to work on integrating feminist pedagogy into their practice (Capobianco, 2002, 2007). As she described it,

> The teachers engaged in systematic, self-critical inquiry of their own practice and joined 8 other science teachers to engage in collaborative conversations about the nature of science, science teaching, and science education as a way of coming to a better understanding of how science can be taught for a more diverse group of students.
>
> (Capobianco, 2007, p. 1)

Capobianco viewed action research as an inquiry-based, self-reflective, collaborative, and emancipatory process. For the focus of this project, the emancipatory aspects dealt with the wicked problem of gender in science education. This was done through meetings every three weeks at Capobianco's home where they ate dinner and engaged in conversations about teaching science for all students. The conversations, which she found were productive and meaningful, helped the science teachers to clarify problems they identified in their search to engage students who had been marginalized in science. They reviewed literature on feminist pedagogy and individually reflected on it through journal writing. The reflection continued communally and collaboratively in the group meetings as the science teachers developed action plans and tried out the strategies with their students. Capobianco saw how during all parts of this process the science teachers assisted one another in "clarifying, justifying, and evaluating their own educational situations through ongoing conversations" (Capobianco, 2007, p. 8).

Capobianco, who had been one of Allan's doctoral students at the University of Massachusetts Amherst, built on his work by using the Enhanced Normal Practice (ENP) model of D-CAR with the science teachers. Through their conversations and enactment of their action research plans, the group uncovered contextual factors and tensions, including the structures of schooling such as daily schedules, teaching assignments, mandated curricula, and high-stakes testing. Capobianco (2007) saw how the teachers worked on transforming their beliefs about science teaching and learning as they successfully devised and implemented inclusive teaching methods. Their transformation combined with their desire to integrate feminist pedagogy into their practice helped to clarify and enhance their beliefs about teaching science and making it accessible for all students. The science teachers along with Capobianco made their action research public in multiple venues, including in a research journal (Capobianco et al., 2006) and one for practitioners (Capobianco et al., 2004).

Including Indigenous Knowledge in Australian Science Curricula

How to include Indigenous knowledge systems in science education is a wicked problem. One aspect of the problem is how science is addressed by teachers epistemologically (Stanley & Brickhouse, 1994) and culturally (Aikenhead, 2001). The epistemological problem resides in the differences between what counts as knowledge in the different systems and how knowledge is developed. It can also be viewed as a cultural problem in that science can be thought of as a set of cultural beliefs that is a subculture of the culture of the Global North. This suggests that to learn science is to assimilate into the culture of science. This requires a type of border crossing that is difficult for students who are part of the Global North culture, and can be even much more so for those from Indigenous groups (Aikenhead & Michell, 2011). Both the epistemological and cultural aspects of including Indigenous knowledge in the classroom are problematic for science teachers. Many of them strongly believe there is only one type of science, and other ways of knowing are orthogonal to it. This can result in them attempting to enculturate all students in the value system of Global North science (Aikenhead, 2001).

This wicked problem is addressed in the Australian National Curriculum with several Cross-Curricular Priorities (CCPs), including one that focuses on Aboriginal and Torres Strait Islander Histories and Cultures. The purposes of this CCP are that Aboriginal and Torres Strait Islander students are able to see themselves, their identities and their cultures reflected in the curriculum … [and that it] is designed for all students to engage in reconciliation, respect and recognition of the world's oldest continuous living cultures.

(ACARA, 2022)

For science, the CCP stated students ought to have the opportunity to learn about Aboriginal and Torres Strait Islanders' long standing knowledge and knowledge traditions developed through observation, prediction and hypothesis, testing, and generalizing about the use of food and natural materials, navigation, and sustainability.

In response to the CCP, Renee Baynes (2016) collaborated with five secondary school science teachers and three critical friends who self-identified as Indigenous people to consider how to develop practices inclusive of Indigenous knowledge. Baynes described the process as participatory action research (PAR) but did not describe what she meant by the term. However, what becomes clear in reading her article is the major activity that occurred when the group met was to reflect individually and collaboratively about their beliefs about the inclusion of Indigenous knowledge in science classes. She noted several concerns were raised by the science teachers through their discussions. One was clearly connected to the issue of cultural border crossings, which was how to make the teaching respectful and meaningful for all students, including avoiding tokenism and "stepping on cultural toes." A second was epistemological: the science teachers wondered how they could make sense of the different ways of knowing, such as the multilayered nature of Indigenous science as compared to the reductionism of Global North science. Finally, as is almost always the case, they were concerned about how they would find the time to develop new teaching strategies.

The major outcome of the action research group was to develop a "Collective Vision for the Inclusion of Indigenous Knowledges in Science Education" through generative dialogue. To Baynes (2016) this was accomplished in dialogue among peers, some of whom were from other schools, which added to the reflective nature of the action research to promote understanding of each other's positions, beliefs, and contexts. She added that the teachers' personal engagement with the issues and dialogue led them to come to consensus on what is necessary to engage with the issues relevant to including Indigenous knowledge in the science curriculum.

Facing Neoliberalism in Self-organized Science Teacher Communities

Betzabé Torres-Olave and Paulina Bravo González (2021) wrote this article while they were both doctoral students studying science teacher communities and PD. They both had been members of self-organized science teacher communities in Chile before beginning their doctoral studies. To them, a self-organized community is one that arises through the initiative of teachers and teacher educators, rather than being mandated from above. As they demonstrate in their research, open and democratic dialogue is an important aspect of these groups. When they chose to analyze these communities, they decided they would do so through dialogue, thereby having a dialogue about a dialogue.

As can be seen from the title of their article, Torres-Olave and Bravo González (2021) examined the self-organized communities through a critical lens in relation to neoliberalism. Before summarizing the role of conversation in their groups, we believe it is necessary to explain what is meant by neoliberalism. The *Stanford Encyclopedia of Philosophy* summarizes it in this way:

> Neoliberalism holds that a society's political and economic institutions should be robustly liberal and capitalist, but supplemented by a constitutionally limited democracy and a modest welfare state. Neoliberals endorse liberal rights and the free-market economy to protect freedom and promote economic prosperity. Neoliberals are broadly democratic, but stress the limitations of democracy as much as its necessity. And while neoliberals typically think government should provide social insurance and public goods, they are skeptical of the regulatory state, extensive government spending, and government-led countercyclical policy.
>
> (Vallier, 2021)

Torres-Olave and Bravo González draw upon the literature on neoliberalism in science education to show how it leads to a false dichotomy between knowledge producers and consumers, and the deprofessionalization of teachers through mandated curricula and high-stakes external examinations. They see self-organized science teacher groups where dialogue is the primary mode of interaction as sites of hope within the neoliberal context.

To Torres-Olave and Bravo González (2021), to engage in dialogue is to talk about issues for particular purposes, such as social and political ones that require the examination of social relations, power, and cultural traditions. What happens in the dialogue depends on what people say, the location of their meetings, how they position themselves, the gestures they use, and all other activity or work related to the group's goals or purposes. They also argue there are at least two dimensions of dialogue: one that is valuable for its role in developing cognitive abilities and conceptual tools; and the other that leads to a revision in our self-understanding.

When she was a science teacher, Bravo González was a member of PRETeC (Profesores Reflexionando por una Educación Transformadora en Ciencias (Teachers Reflecting for a Transformational Science Education)), which was established in 2013. The group engaged in issues such as the image of science teachers, the importance of science for their lives and the lives of their students, and their conceptualization of science education in Chile. The way they shared their practice within the group was through discussions and reflections about lesson stories, which are written descriptions of individual teachers' classroom activities. These stories have been collected in a book published in Chile (PRETeC, 2018). Bravo González described how one of these stories was used in PRETeC:

> a lesson story shared in one session was related to the consensus that Pluto was no longer a planet and the students did not understand why that decision was taken; in that session, the group reflected on the nature of science and gave ideas to the lesson story's author to keep developing that understanding of how the knowledge is built. One idea was to develop with the students a biographic review of the people involved in the classification of the planets, to understand where, how and who were those people.
>
> (p. 1055)

Torres-Olave provides a description of how the group of nine physics teachers, to which she belonged, started in 2012. They started with a water rocket activity, and shared ideas about how they would introduce the concepts, the design, and so on. This became a yearly activity, which led the teachers to talk about other things, such as science communication, public engagement, and collaboration with pre-service teachers. The teachers saw it as a way of refreshing themselves, and engaging in real collaboration using the local area as a living laboratory. They reported to Torres-Olave they knew more about pedagogy and the curriculum due to being a part of the group. They attributed this to engaging in collaborative conversations in a trusting environment. Overall, the collaboration was "transformative since it goes against the traditional lone working and encourages reflection that is then translated into actions" (Torres-Olave & Bravo González, 2021, p. 1056).

Torres-Olave and Bravo González (2021) summarize the effects of science teachers' participation in self-organized communities as a shift in the culture of common practice away from the culture of silence deepened by the neoliberal politics of schooling. Groups like the ones they participated in develop a culture built around the "necessity of talking" and an "urgency to say the words that go in line with the very nature of the teaching profession: a dialogic dynamic" (Torres-Olave & Bravo González, 2021, p. 1058). In these collective spaces, teachers are able to create the personal views and collective purposes that become sites of hope for science education.

Elevating Discussions About Equity in STEM Education

Our final example is of work that Katie did with STEM teachers in Florida (Laux, 2023), which we touched upon in Chapter 5. She engaged a group of science, robotics, and engineering teachers in a PLC in which they engaged in D-CAR to investigate equity issues in their classrooms. She met with the teachers virtually once a month during the 2021–2022 school year, and worked with one of the teachers outside of the meetings with whom she took a six-week diversity, equity, and inclusion (DEI) training. This led to many conversations about how to improve the quality of the dialogue during the monthly meetings. In addition to the Zoom meetings (https://zoom.us), the teachers used apps such as Microsoft Whiteboard (https://www.microsoft.com/en-us/microsoft-365/microsoft-whiteboard/digital-whiteboard-app), Padlet (https://padlet.com), and Menti (https://www.menti.com) to structure their conversations.

At the beginning of the school year Katie noted the teachers had difficulty even seeing how a discussion about equity could be incorporated into their STEM lessons. By the end of the year, their conversations turned to solutions to make equitable experiences for students a reality. They recognized students' backgrounds or experiences play a role in what they do in school, and made their lessons more inclusive by increasing parent involvement, utilizing students' funds of knowledge, incorporating student notebook reflections, and integrating choice boards to appreciate student differences in learning styles. Overall, through the use of dialogic methods, the STEM teachers became more comfortable with equity issues and began to engage in verbal dialogue with each other. They also took on more leadership roles in the group and had more voice in the D-CAR process.

Summary

Our primary goal in this chapter was to provide readers with examples of how dialogue and conversations are used in science teacher action research. As can be seen in each of the examples, even when the action research was described as being conventional, the collaboration among the teachers and with facilitators in group meetings was highlighted as where knowledge and understanding were shared and constructed. We also wanted to demonstrate that action research using dialogic methods happens around the world. Our examples came from the US, Canada, New Zealand, South Africa, Australia, and Chile. We're sure there are other examples we didn't have access to because we were limited to English language publications. We also wanted to show how dialogical forms of action research are already being used to address wicked educational problems including teaching controversial topics, inequity, curriculum distribution, gender issues, the incorporation of Indigenous knowledge into science education, and the effects of neoliberalism on the teaching and learning of science. We hope these examples provide our readers with the inspiration needed to make use of D-CAR, and to begin the difficult work of addressing wicked educational problems in science education.

Note

1 Note: NSTA no longer has this position statement on its website. However, it was published in its entirety in the *Iowa Science Teachers Journal*. Our citation is to that version.

References

ACARA (2022). *Aboriginal and Torres Strait Islander histories and cultures (Version 8.4)*. Australian Curriculum, Assessment and Reporting Authority (ACARA). Retrieved July 22 from https://www.australiancurriculum.edu.au/f-10-curriculum/cross-curriculum-priorities/aboriginal-and-torres-strait-islander-histories-and-cultures/.

Aikenhead, G., & Michell, H. (2011). *Bridging cultures: Indigenous and scientific ways of knowing nature*. Toronto, ON: Pearson Canada.

Aikenhead, G. S. (2001). Integrating Western and Aboriginal sciences: Cross-cultural science teaching. *Research in Science Education*, 31(3), 337–355. doi:10.1023/A:1013151709605.

Baynes, R. (2016). Teachers' attitudes to including Indigenous knowledges in the Australian science curriculum. *Australian Journal of Indigenous Education*, 45(1), 80–90. doi:10.1017/jie.2015.29.

Berkheimer, G. D., Bybee, R. W., Donnellan, K. M., Hurd, P. D., Maxwell, D. E., Peterson, R., & Pratt, H. (1983). An NSTA Position Statement: Science–Technology–Society: Science education for the 1980s. *Iowa Science Teachers Journal*, 20(2), 16–20. https://scholarworks.uni.edu/cgi/viewcontent.cgi?article=1788&context=istj.

Capobianco, B. M. (2002). *Making science accessible through collaborative science teacher action research on feminist pedagogy*, Thesis (Ed D), University of Massachusetts at Amherst.

Capobianco, B. M. (2007). Science teachers' attempts at integrating feminist pedagogy through collaborative action research. *Journal of Research in Science Teaching*, 44(1), 1–32. doi:10.1002/tea.20120.

Capobianco, B., Horowitz, R., Canuel-Browne, D., & Trimarchi, R. (2004). Action research for teachers. *The Science Teacher*, 71(3), 48–53.

Capobianco, B. M., Lincoln, S., Canuel-Browne, D., & Trimarchi, R. (2006). Examining the experiences of three generations of teacher researchers through collaborative science teacher inquiry. *Teacher Education Quarterly* (Summer), 61–78.

Cochran-Smith, M., & Lytle, S. (2009). Inquiry as stance: Practitioner research in the next generation. *Review of Research in Education*, 24(1), 249–305. doi:10.3102/0091732X024001249.

Fazio, X. (2009). Teacher development using group discussion and reflection. *Reflective Practice*, 10(4), 529–541. doi:10.1080/14623940903138407.

Fazio, X., & Melville, W. (2008). Science teacher development through collaborative action research. *Teacher Development*, 12(3), 193–209. doi:10.1080/13664530802259222.

Feldman, A., & Capobianco, B. (2008). Teacher learning of technology enhanced formative assessment. *Journal of Science Education and Technology*, 17(1), 82–99. doi:10.1007/s10956-007-9084-0.

France, B., Mora, H. A., & Bay, J. L. (2012). Changing perspectives: Exploring a pedagogy to examine other perspectives about stem cell research. *International Journal of Science Education*, 34(5), 803–824. doi:10.1080/09500693.2011.630427.

Kumar, D. D., & Berlin, D. F. (1993). Science–Technology–Society policy implementation in the USA: A literature review. *The Review of Education*, 15(1), 73–83. doi:10.1080/0098559930150111.

Laux, K. (2023). Elevating discussions about equity in STEM education. Poster presented at the Annual Conference of the Association for Science Teacher Education, Salt Lake City, UT.

McNiff, J. (2006). *Teaching as learning: An action research approach.* New York and Abingdon, UK: Routledge.

Nelson, T. H. (2009). Teachers' collaborative inquiry and professional growth: Should we be optimistic? *Science Education*, 93(3), 548–580. doi:10.1002/sce.20302.

O'Donoghue, R. B., & McNaught, C. (1991). Environmental education: The development of a curriculum through 'grass-roots' reconstructive action. *International Journal of Science Education*, 13(4), 391–404. doi:10.1080/0950069910130403.

Oulton, C., Dillon, J., & Grace, M. M. (2004). Reconceptualizing the teaching of controversial issues. *International Journal of Science Education*, 26(4), 411–423. doi:10.1080/0950069032000072746.

Pedretti, E. (1996). Learning about science, technology, and society (STS) through an action research project: Co-constructing an issues-based model for STS education. *School Science and Mathematics*, 96(8), 432–440. doi:10.1111/j.1949-8594.1996. tb15866.x.

PRETeC (2018). *Navegamos pese a todo. Reflexionando para transformar la educación en ciencias.* Pontificia Universidad Católica de Valparaíso. https://www.researchgate. net/profile/Paulina-Bravo/publication/330324987_Navegamos_pese_a_todo_ PRETeC/links/5c38fb17299bf12be3c13ea3/Navegamos-pese-a-todo-PRETeC.pdf.

Rearick, M., & Feldman, A. (1999). Orientations, product, reflections: A framework for understanding action research. *Teaching and Teacher Education*, 15(4), 333–350. doi:10.1016/S0742-051X(98)00053-5.

Shor, I., & Freire, P. (1987). *A pedagogy for liberation: Dialogues on transforming education.* Westport, CT: Bergin & Garvey Publishers.

Stanley, W. B., & Brickhouse, N. W. (1994). Multiculturalism, universalism, and science education. *Science Education*, 78(4), 387–398. doi:10.1002/sce.3730780405 and http://silk.library.umass.edu:2048/login?url=http://search.ebscohost.com/ login.aspx?direct=true&db=eric&AN=EJ493813&site=ehost-live&scope=site.

Subramaniam, K. (2010). Understanding changes in teacher roles through collaborative action research. *Journal of Science Teacher Education*, 21(8), 937–951. doi:10.1007/ s10972-010-9217-9.

Tobin, K., & Tippins, D. J. (1996). Metaphors as seeds for conceptual change and the improvement of science teaching. *Science Education*, 80(6), 711–730. doi:10.1002/ (SICI)1098-237X(199611)80:6<711::AID-SCE5>3.0.CO;2-M.

Torres-Olave, B., & Bravo González, P. (2021). Facing neoliberalism through dialogic spaces as sites of hope in science education: experiences of two self-organised communities. *Cultural Studies of Science Education*, 16(4), 1047–1067. doi:10.1007/ s11422–11021–10042-y.

Vallier, K. (2021). Neoliberalism. In E. N. Zalta (Ed.), *The Stanford encyclopedia of philosophy.* Stanford, CA: Metaphysics Research Lab, Stanford University. https://plato. stanford.edu/archives/sum2021/entries/neoliberalism.

10 Afterword

Most likely you are reading this because you've come to the end of our book. We hope it has led you to think and act differently about the ways that dialogic collaborative action research (D-CAR) can help you and your colleagues to improve science teaching and learning, and add to our knowledge of the field. We also hope it has helped you to become aware of and begin to work to mitigate the wicked problems that affect your practice.

When we proposed the idea of this book to our editor at Taylor & Francis, we wrote it is primarily aimed at science teacher educators, preservice and inservice teacher researchers, school district professional development (PD) staff, and university education faculty. For science teacher educators, we envisioned them using our ideas in their work with preservice and inservice teachers. There have been attempts over many years to incorporate action research into preservice teacher education. This would usually occur during a practicum, internship, or student teaching placement. While it is important for these future teachers to learn to reflect on their practice, engagement in conventional action research can be onerous given they are novices who are learning to plan and deliver lessons, and manage student behaviors. D-CAR provides a mechanism that can be used to structure reflection and enculturate preservice science teachers into a community of practitioners collaborating with one another as they wrestle with problems, dilemmas, and dissonances of practice.

As already mentioned in our list of who this book is aimed at, university education faculty were included in addition to science teacher educators. While science teacher educators are often university education faculty, it is not necessarily the case. There are people who engage in the practice of teacher education without being academic researchers. For those practitioners of science teacher education, whether or not they are academic researchers, our hope is they engage in dialogic, collaborative groups to share and construct knowledge of teacher preparation, and to communicate it throughout the field. For academic researchers of science teaching and teachers, we see their establishment of D-CAR groups as a way to both uncover new knowledge of teaching and learning, but also become part of the collaborative groups as co-action researchers.

DOI: 10.4324/9781003307174-10

For the most part our book has focused on the use of D-CAR by inservice science teachers. The vignettes and examples we shared illustrated how groups of science teachers can come together to identify the issues they face in their day-to-day practice, as well as the wicked problems that permeate their educational situations. As we've shown and argued throughout this text, D-CAR can be embedded in teachers' practice in a way that makes it sustainable. We've also pointed out the importance for science teachers to share the knowledge and understanding they construct and uncover with others beyond their group. It has been too long that teachers have not had access to the remarkable innovations developed by their colleagues. In addition to stagnating the field, it has given power to outsiders to take on the role of knowledge producers and relegated teachers to consumers of knowledge. It is time for education to be a knowledge democracy.

We would like to see school district professional development staff acknowledge the knowledge and wisdom of practicing science teachers. D-CAR incorporates all the tenets of good PD, and does more by allowing teachers to construct and share the knowledge they demonstrated works in the classroom. This would require a shift from delivering PD to partnering with teachers in the improvement of science teaching and learning in their educational situations. It would also require PD staff to become facilitators and critical friends, and to possibly produce a cadre of skilled facilitators. Too often PD is top down, focusing on the problems identified by administrators and policy makers, rather than by the teachers who have deep knowledge of the needs of their students, schools, and communities.

Finally, our hope is that this book will be used by science teachers, science teacher educators, and others throughout the world, not only the USA. It is clear to us, and most likely for you, that our book is US-centric. We have tried to include international perspectives, and have included examples from around the world in Chapter 9. But science teaching and learning is very much influenced by local, regional, and national conditions. For those of you who are reading this book outside of the USA, our hope is that we have made our writing broad enough to be usable for your educational situation.

Index

Note: Page numbers in **bold** refer to tables and page numbers in *italic* refer to figures.

Achiam, Marianne 48, 51
Action Learning, Action Research
  Association (ALARA) 123
action research: approach to 4–6;
  characteristics 13–16; as collaborative
  14–15; and constructivism 16–18; as
  cyclical 15–16, *15*; defining 12–13;
  done by practitioners on and in their
  practice 14; history 11–12; making
  public 7, 16, 33, 114–125; purposes of
  13–14; in science education 18–24 *see
  also* collaborative action research;
  conventional action research; dialogic
  collaborative action research (D-CAR)
Action Research Network of the
  Americas (ARNA) 123
action research networks 123–124
administrative support 105, 107, 109, 111
Aloni, Nimrod 35–36
Alsultan, Jawaher 2–3, 17–18, 23, 34,
  48, 56, 72, 85
Altrichter, Herbert 2, 64
analytic discourse 64–65, 66, 67
archival data 88, 94
Aristotle 120
associations, science teacher 122
Australian Curriculum, Assessment and
  Reporting Authority (ACARA) 138

Baird, J.R. 22
Barber, Mark 72
barriers to implementing conventional
  action research 105–112; administrative support 105, 107, 109, 111;
  deprofessionalization of teaching
  105–107; difficulties in changing one's
  practice 109–110; issues with

professional development programs
  110–111; time constraints 108–109
Bascia, N. 106
Baynes, Renee 22, 56, 138
Bereiter, Carl 36
Bergmark, Ulrika 76
Berkheimer, G.D. 135
Bildung 59, 60
Borjas, Mónica 20, 23
brainstorming 68, 84
Bravo González, Paulina 56, 138–140
Brenner, Mary 23–24
Buckingham, Burdette 11
buzz groups 68

Cammarota, Julio 21, 74, 75
Capobianco, Brenda 20, 21–22, 56, 116,
  117, 129, 136–137
case studies, D-CAR 129–141; addressing non-wicked problems 129–132;
  addressing wicked problems 132–141
change of practice, difficulties in enacting
  109–110
characteristics of action research 13–16
Cheung, Rebecca 116
Chimwayange, C. 74
Claims, Evidence, Reasoning (CER)
  framework 58, 85, 89, 93, 94
climate change education 4, 49–50, 59
Cochran-Smith, Marilyn 35, 64,
  131, 132
coding 97, 99, 100; qualitative data
  100–102
collaboration 31–33, 56–57, 74
collaborative action research 14–15, 20,
  22, 33–35, 129–130 *see also* dialogic
  collaborative action research (D-CAR)

Collaborative Action Research Network (CARN) 123
communities of practice 34–35, 38, 72, 124
Compliment–Connect–Comment–Question 67
concept maps 68
constructivism, action research and 16–18
controversial topics, addressing 48–50, 133
conventional action research 5, 7–8, 37–38; barriers to implementing 105–112; data analysis 95–103; data collection plans 93–94; data types 85–86, 87–92; informed consent 94–95; ladder of inference 86–87, *86*; research questions 84–85; starting points 83–84
conversations as research 7, 35–36; methods for engaging in 57–73
Cook, B.G. 119
cool feedback 72
Corey, Stephen 12
Costa, Arthur 77, 78
COVID-19 pandemic 3, 18, 34, 72
credibility 102
critical friends 75, 77–78, 89, 138
Cross-Cultural Priorities (CCPs) 137–138
curriculum 44–45, 46, 47, 106–107; center-periphery model of development 134, *135*; Decolonisation of the Curriculum Project 24; development of science 22–23; dissemination 134–135; Indigenous knowledge in science 24, 45, 137–138
cycle, action research 15–16, *15*

data: analysis 95–103; collection plans 93–94; triangulation 102–103; types 85–86, 87–92
de Beer, Josef 24
Decolonisation of the Curriculum Project 24
defining action research 12–13
deprofessionalization of teaching 105–107, 139
descriptive statistics 97, *98, 99*
Dewey, John 12, 32
dialogic collaborative action research (D-CAR) 5–6, 36–38; addressing non-wicked problems 129–132; addressing wicked problems 6, 50, 51, 118,

132–141; administrative support for 105, 107, 109, 111; case studies 129–141; collaboration 31–33, 56–57; critical friends 75, 77–78, 89, 138; engaging with 6–8; establishing a group 6–7, 55–56; facilitating teachers to change practice 107, 110, 111; facilitators 75–77, 89, 111, 145; including student voices 73–75; making public 7, 16, 33, 59, 114–125; methods for creating conversations 57–73; mitigating effects of time constraints 109; nature of dialogue 35–36; preservice teachers and 144; reasons to focus on 31; regaining teacher autonomy through 107; sharing research within group 121–122
Dialogos Method 59–61, *60*
DiCicco, Michael 84
digital game-based learning (DGBL) 3, 18
Dillon, Justin 48
Dimmock, Clive 32

Eilks, Ingo 19, 22, 23, 114
Elbow, Peter 65
elevator pitches 84
Elliott, John 12–13, 15, 32, 37, 67, 117
Enhanced Normal Practice (ENP) 57–59, 137
equity: D-CAR group to investigate issues of equity in STEM education 63–64, 140–141; in science teaching and learning 23–24, 50
evidence-based practice (EBP) 119
Excel 96–97

facilitators 75–77, 89, 111, 145
facts 87
Fals-Borda, Orlando 12, 21, 23, 118–119
Fazio, Xavier 19, 56, 75, 117, 129, 130–131
feedback 72, 77, 78, 114
Feldman, Allan 1–2, 4, 5, 7, 11, 12, 13, 14, 15, 17, 18, 19, 20, 21, 22, 23, 31, 32, 33, 34, 35, 36, 37, 38, 49, 56, 57, 58, 59, 63, 64, 65, 66, 67, 70, 72, 75, 77, 78, 86, 90, 92, 93, 102, 108, 109–110, 117–118, 120, 121, 130, 133
feminist pedagogy, integrating 136–137
Fine, Michelle 21, 74, 75
fishbone-analysis 68, *69*

focus groups 91
force-field analysis 68
France, Bev 56, 133
free writing 65
Freire, Paulo 21, 118, 134

gap activity 65, 83
generated data 88–92
Glackin, Melissa 48
Global Bildung Network 59
global climate change (GCC) 4, 49–50
Global North 118, 119, 120, 137
Global South 118–119, 120
Goodnough, Karen 23, 68, 75, 76–77, 117
groups, D-CAR: challenge of maintaining 111; starting 6–7, 55–56

Hawamdeh, Asma 20, 22
Helskog, Guro 59, 60
history of action research 11–12
holistic: data analysis 100; grading 100
Hollingsworth, Sandra 35, 37
Horizon Research 89
Horn, Ilana 36
Human Research Protection Program 95

Indigenous knowledge: in knowledge democracy 119; in science curriculum 24, 45, 137–138; in YPAR 74–75
inferences 87
informed consent 94–95
Institutional Review Boards (IRB) 94–95
interactive action research 20–21
Internet, publishing on 124–125
interview protocols 91
interviews 90–91

Johnston, Adam 66
Jones, Rufus 50
journal clubs 63
journals, publishing in 59, 124
journey maps 69–72, 70, 71

Kallick, Bena 77, 78
Kane, Britnie 36
Kane, R.G. 74
Kemmis, S. 12, 13, 14, 15, 17, 18, 19, 20, 21, 23
knowledge: action research and construction of 16–17; democracy 118–120; importance of sharing 5–6, 114–115; science teachers as producers of 14, 115–116, 135, 145; status of teachers'

vs. university researchers' 32, 116, 119, 120 *see also* Indigenous knowledge
Kolko, Jon 47
Koshy, Valsa 14, 15

ladder of inference 86–87, 86
Landemore, H. 5, 120
language in collaborative groups 36
Laudonia, Ivano 19, 20, 21, 22, 23
Laux, Katie 3–4, 56, 59, 62, 63–64, 73–74, 74, 108, 111, 140–141
leadership, teacher 116
lesson study 61–62, 62
Lewin, Kurt 11, 37
Lincoln, Y.S. 17, 102
Lytle, Susan 35, 64, 131, 132

Making Sense of Learning (MSL) project 74
McIntyre, A. 74
McNaught, C. 56, 134–135
McNiff, J. 15, 18, 19, 21, 31, 36, 131
Melville, Wayne 22, 56, 117, 129, 130, 131
memos 99–100
Mentz, Elsa 24
methods for creating dialogic conversations 57–73
Microsoft Excel 96–97
mind maps 69
Minstrell, Jim 22
Mitchell, I.J. 22
Mitchell, J. 22
mixed-methods research 103

Nation, Molly 4, 49, 59
National Science Education Standards 44
National Science Teachers Association (NSTA) 122, 124, 135
Nelson, Tamara 56, 129, 131–132
neoliberalism 138–140
Next Generation Science Standards (NGSS) 46
Noffke, Susan 11, 13, 19, 115, 116, 117, 125
nominal data 97
non-parametric tests 97
nonverbal communication 63
null hypothesis 95
Nyhof-Young, Joyce 24

observation protocol 89
observations 87, 88–90

O'Donoghue, R.B. 56, 134–135
online: action research and online
teaching in COVID-19 pandemic 3,
18, 34, 72; conversations 63, 72–73,
140–141; publishing 124–125
Oostveen, Roland van 75, 76, 77
oral inquiry processes 35
ordinal data 97

participatory action research (PAR)
21–22, 90; in Latin America 118–119;
youth participatory action research
(YPAR) 74–75
Paul, Rand 49
PechaKucha presentations 121
pedagogical content knowledge
(PCK) 115
Pedretti, Erminia 56, 135–136
Peña-Leyva, Fátima De la 20, 23
personal purposes, sharing research for
116–117
Photovoice 84, 90
Physics Teachers Action Research Group
(PTARG) 2, 35, 57–59, *57*, 77, 111
Piaget, Jean 16
Planning-Programming-Budgeting
Systems (PPBS) 44
Planning, Realization, and Assessment
(PRA) framework 18
political purposes, sharing research for
117–118
Posch, Peter 64
practical reasoning 59–60
presentation software 121
presentations 121, 122
preservice teachers and D-CAR 144
PRETeC 139–140
Prezi 121
profession, teaching as a: deprofessionalization of teaching 105–107, 139;
status of 32, 115, 116
professional development (PD) 23, 32,
107, 116, 145; digital game-based
learning (DGBL) 3, 18; programs 3,
110–111
professional learning communities (PLCs)
32, 63–64, 122; case study 131–132
professional purposes, sharing research
for 115–116
Programme for International Student
Assessment (PISA) 46
progressive dialogue 36
Project for Enhancing Effective Learning
(PEEL) 22

public, making action research 7, 16, 33,
114–125; to contribute to knowledge
democracy 118–120; importance of
114–115; methods for 120–124; for
personal purposes 116–117; for
political purposes 117–118; for
professional purposes 115–116
publishing: on Internet 124–125; in
journals 59, 124
purposes of action research 13–14

qualitative data 88; analysis 97–102
quantitative data 87–88
questionnaires 91–92
questions, research 84–85

Rearick, Mary 117–118, 130, 133
reconnaissance 15, 37, 67
recordings 88–89
reflective practice 38, 110, 111, 131,
133, 137
reform: initiatives in science teaching 44,
107; systemic 47
Reformed Teaching Observation
Protocol (RTOP) 89
Reiss, Michael 48
report writing conventions 121
reports of action research 121
research questions 84–85
Rittel, Horst 6, 43, 44, 45, 46, 47
rubrics 93, 97, 100

Saldaña, Johnny 97, 99
science education: action research 18–24;
reform of 44, 47, 107; standards
44–45, 46, 47, 106–107; wicked
problems in 44, 47–50
science teacher associations 122
Science-Technology-Society (STS)
Education 135–136
scientific inquiry and the nature of science
130–131
scoring rubrics 93, 97
self-organized science teacher communities 56, 138–140
semi-professions 106
Settlage, John 66
SHOWED framework 90
Shulman, Lee 115
social justice in science teaching and
learning 23–24, 31, 117–118; YPAR
to promote 75
societal and educational problems, wicked
44, 50

software, presentation 121
speech in collaborative groups 36
standards, science education 44–45, 46, 47, 106–107
starting point: for research 83–84; speeches 66–67, 84
statistical analysis 95–97, *98, 99*
stem cell research, engaging with 133
Stenhouse, Lawrence 6, 12, 13, 16, 33, 38, 114–115
Stewart-Mitchell, Jennifer 67
student participation, hierarchy of 73–74, *74*
student voice, including 73–75
Subramaniam, Karthigeyan 56, 129–130
surveys and questionnaires 91–92
SWOT analysis 68

t-tests 96–97
taking an inquiry stance 131–132
teacher-centered action research 21
teaching to the test 108
technical action research 19–20
technology, science teachers use of 129–130
testing: difference between sample-sets 95–97, **96**; high-stakes 45, 47, 64, 106–107, 108, 139
Thompson, Marissa 67
Thoughts, Lingering Questions, and Epiphanies (TQE) 67
Tikunoff, William 32
time constraints 38, 108–109
Torres-Olave, Betzabé 56, 138–140

transcripts 100
triangulation 102–103

validity 102
Vallier, K. 139
Vangrieken, Katrien 33
venture-vexations 66
Visvanathan, S. 120
Vygotsky, Lev 16

Wang, Carolyn 84, 90
Ward, B.A. 32
warm feedback 72
Webber, Melvin 6, 43, 44, 45, 46, 47
Wells, Gordon 14, 20, 37
Wenger, Etienne 20, 63
Wenger-Traynor, Etienne and Wenger-Traynor, Beverly 34, 35
wicked problems 6, 31, 43–51; characteristics 44–47; D-CAR to address 6, 50, 51, 118, 132–141; in science education 44, 47–50
Wilcoxon Signed Rank Test 97
Williamson, Janee 72
Wipro Science Education Fellowship (SEF) program 56, 66
Woo, A. 49
workshops 122
writing conventions, report 121
written consent 95

youth participatory action research (YPAR) 74–75

Printed in the United States
by Baker & Taylor Publisher Services